Anonymous

**A Sketch of South Australia for the Melbourne International Exhibition**

Anonymous

**A Sketch of South Australia for the Melbourne International Exhibition**

ISBN/EAN: 9783337319960

Printed in Europe, USA, Canada, Australia, Japan

Cover: Foto ©Thomas Meinert / pixelio.de

More available books at **www.hansebooks.com**

# A SKETCH

OF

# South Australia

FOR THE

# MELBOURNE INTERNATIONAL EXHIBITION,

## 1880.

*Published by direction of the Royal Commissioners for South Australia.*

## WITH MAPS AND STATISTICAL DIAGRAMS.

Adelaide:

E. SPILLER, GOVERNMENT PRINTER, NORTH-TERRACE.

1880.

# MAP
## OF
## THE AUSTRALIAN COLONIES.

SURVEYOR GENERAL'S OFFICE ADELAIDE

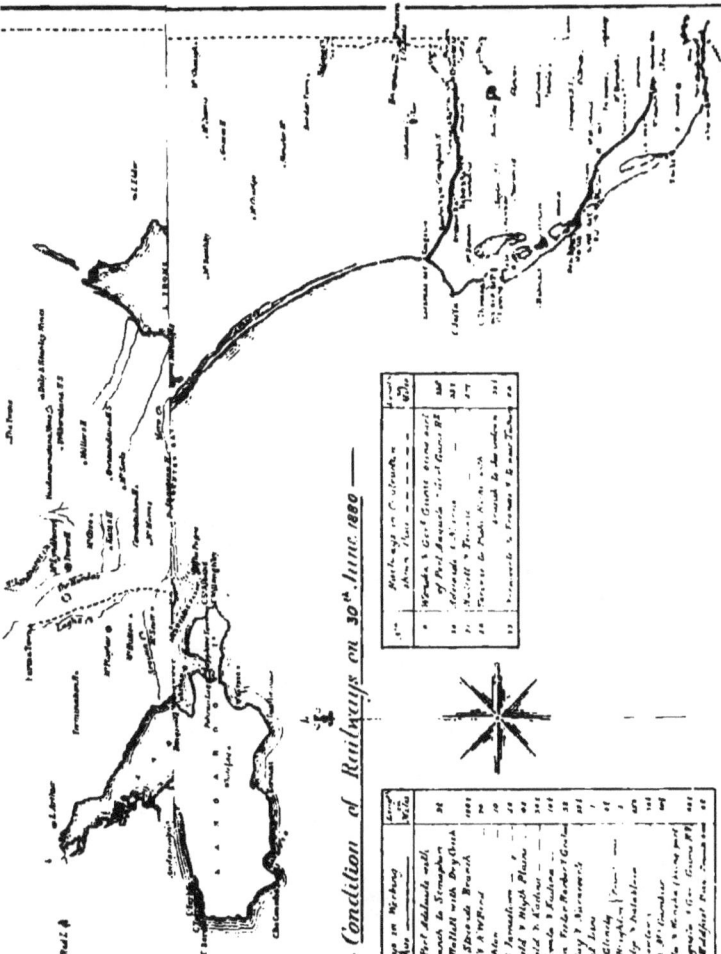

MAP
Shewing
LINES OF RAILWAYS
in
SOUTH AUSTRALIA
1880

— Condition of Railways on 30th June 1880 —

# CONTENTS.

# Chap. I.—General Description.

## 1.—*Position and Extent.*

A GLANCE at the accompanying map shows that, in spite of her name, South Australia occupies the central portion of the Australian Continent. Lying between 12° and 38° S. lat., and 129° and 141° E. long., the colony extends from the Indian to the Southern Ocean, and is bounded on the east by Queensland, New South Wales, and Victoria; on the west by Western Australia. Roughly defined, her territory is 2,000 miles long by 500 miles wide, and has an area of over 903,000 square miles—about ten times that of Great Britain.

With the exception of a small settlement on the northern coast (to which a separate chapter will be given) colonisation has hitherto been confined to an area of about a quarter of a million square miles, in the southern part of the colony; and it is consequently to this that the remarks made about South Australia in the following pages must be understood to apply. A portion of the colony still remains unexplored.

## 2.—*Physical Features.*

For present purposes of description, the southern portion of the province may be divided into six districts:—1, Metropolitan; 2, the South-East; 3, the Northern Areas; 4, the Far North; 5, Yorke's Peninsula; 6, Port Lincoln.

1. THE METROPOLITAN lies to the east of St. Vincent's Gulf, and may be divided into three parts —the coast-plain, the eastern plains, and the mountain ranges between.

The coast-plain extends from Cape Jervis to Port Wakefield, and varies in width from a mere point in the south to about thirty miles in the County of Gawler. Immediately south of Port Wakefield is the Thirty Mile Scrub, a tract of light soil, formerly much covered with mallee and brushwood. Between this and the hills is the fertile district of Hoyle's Plains. Southward, towards Adelaide, much of the country is under cultivation. South of the capital it becomes hilly, and is very productive; but near Cape Jervis it is in many places coated with low scrub, and grazed by cattle.

The mountain range, to the east of the coast plain, consists of a succession of hills, running north and south, with a mean breadth of about thirty miles. The slopes and valleys, often of great natural beauty, are dotted with townships and homesteads. The southern portion depastures sheep and cattle. In the north, farming is combined with grazing. The whole district is rich in minerals.

The eastern plains, from the mountains to the Murray, are low undulations and flats, generally

covered with scrub growths. Hitherto this country
has been sparsely grazed, but it is gradually being
cleared for agricultural settlement.

2. THE SOUTH-EAST is the name applied to the
district lying south-east of the Murray mouth. Immediately east from the Murray are extensive sandy
mallee and pine scrubs, which are being enclosed and
improved by the depasturing of sheep. Further south,
the Counties of MacDonnell, Robe, and Grey com-
prise agricultural districts. Near Millicent, drainage
works have rendered the land more productive; and
similarly useful works are contemplated over a like
description of country northwards, towards Lacepede
Bay. In the neighborhood of Mount Gambier the
country is picturesque and rich, and English root
crops, hops, and grasses thrive along with wheat.
With the exception of the southernmost corner,
which is of volcanic origin, the common feature of this
district is an alternation of flats and ridges, more or
less timbered, and running parallel to the sea-coast.

3. THE NORTHERN AREAS are agricultural lands
lying east of the upper part of Spencer's Gulf, for the
most part in the Counties of Daly, Stanley, Victoria,
Frome, Dalhousie, and the western parts of Kimberley
and the Burra. Running due north from Port Wakefield is a range of hills known as the Hummocks,
succeeded by the Flinders Range.

4. THE FAR NORTH is the name applied to the
saltbush and myall country, lying north-west, north,

and north-east of Port Augusta. To the north and west is a series of large shallow lakes ; east of these is the Flinders Range. From about thirty miles east of the range to the border are low fertile flats, covered with cotton, salt, and other kindred bushes adapted for sheep. Extensive mineral deposits of copper and iron are found in the neighborhood of the Flinders Range.

5. YORKE'S PENINSULA, lying between gulfs Spencer and St. Vincent, is 120 miles long by twenty broad. In the northern portion are the celebrated copper mines and smelting works of Wallaroo and Moonta. Here the country is flat and scrubby, but to the south there is a large quantity of open wheat-growing land, having portions of low swampy ground interspersed with sheaoak ridges.

6. PORT LINCOLN, of triangular shape, lies west of Spencer's Gulf; the Gawler Ranges running across from east to west form its northern boundary. A belt of sandy and scrubby country, some fifty miles across, stretches out between this range and the sea coast. A number of colonists who combine sheep with wheat farming live along the shore. Settlement has but little penetrated into the central portion of this district.

### 3.—Coast-line and Harbors.

The southern coast-line—over 2,000 miles long—is indented by two deep gulfs, giving access to large agricultural districts in the interior, which, without them, must have remained uncultivated for many years.

Between Cape Northumberland, near the eastern boundary, and Cape Jervis, opposite Kangaroo Island, the country is accessible by Port MacDonnell, Rivoli Bay, Robe, Lacepede Bay, and Port Victor. MacDonnell Bay is connected with Mount Gambier and Penola by a good macadamised road. From Rivoli Bay a railway extends fifty miles eastward to Mount Gambier, and from Lacepede Bay there is also a line reaching into the Tatiara district. At Encounter Bay the Murray empties itself into the sea, but unfortunately the entrance at its mouth is not easily navigable. To meet this obstacle large harbor works are being constructed at Port Victor, which is connected with Goolwa west of the Murray mouth by a light railway, some nine miles long.

West of Cape Jervis are, first, St. Vincent's and then Spencer's Gulf, divided by Yorke's Peninsula. Along their shores are several harbors; most of these have jetties, and some are connected with the interior by railway. The chief shipping places are Port Adelaide and Port Wakefield on St. Vincent's Gulf, and Ports Augusta, Pirie, and Wallaroo on Spencer's Gulf. From all of these railways stretch into the interior, that from Port Augusta being in the direction of a trans-continental line to Port Darwin, on the Indian Ocean.

On the western shore of Spencer's Gulf, towards
the south, is the magnificent harbor of Port Lincoln ;
thence, following the coast towards Western Australia, are several good anchorages, such as Coffin's,
Venus, Streaky, Denial, and Fowler's Bays.

### 4.—Mountains.

The mountains of Australia in no part attain any
great height.  The principal chain in South Australia is the Flinders Range, commencing north of the
head of St. Vincent's Gulf, and running northwards
for several hundred miles as far as Lake Blanche.
The highest peaks are Mounts Remarkable and
Brown, each about 3,200ft.

After a short break the Flinders Range is continued
due south to Port Wakefield by a line of hills called
the Hummocks, and south-east by a continuous line
of ranges running along the eastern side of St.
Vincent's Gulf, as far as Cape Jervis.  The most
important of this group of hills is the Mount Lofty
Range (2,334ft.), forming a pretty background to
the metropolis.

The Flinders Range is practically followed at
intervals by the Mount Nor.-West, Musgrave, Mac-
Donnell, Stuart, Strzelecki, Murchison, and Ash-
burton ranges.  Several prominent points on the
Musgrave and MacDonnell are more than 4,000ft.
above sea level.

## 5.—*Rivers.*

The Murray is the only river worthy of the name—running into the Southern Ocean—within the boundaries of South Australia. The country generally is watered by streams which, in the winter months, attain the proportions of moderate sized rivers, but during the summer are reduced to mere creeks, or a sucession of waterholes.

The Murray from its source, near Mount Kosciusko, after forming a boundary between New South Wales and Victoria, enters South Australia at longitude 141° E., and empties itself into the Southern Ocean at Encounter Bay, having run a distance of about 2,400 miles, nearly 2,000 miles of which are navigable. A shifting sandy bar stretches across the entrance at its mouth.

## 6.—*Lakes.*

Towards the mouth of the Murray are the large and beautiful freshwater lakes known as Lakes Alexandrina and Albert, abounding in waterfowl and freshwater fish, and skirted by grassy banks, forming bays and headlands of great beauty. Other lakes in the interior are mostly brackish—varying in size according to the season. Of these a series of fourteen lie northerly and north-westerly from Port Augusta, the largest being Lakes Eyre and Gairdner. For 80 miles along the coast, S.E. of the Murray Mouth, is the Coorong backwater from the sea; and there is a chain of saltwater lakes parallel to the coast between Robe and MacDonnell Bay.

### 7.—*Geological Features.*

The geological features of the colony are but very imperfectly known, no systematic examination of the country having yet been made. Of the three great epochs into which the world's præ-adamite history has been divided, only the palæozoic and the tertiary rocks are known to exist in this colony, the secondary rocks having hitherto escaped observation—if they are present at all.

The mountain chain which practically commences at Cape Jervis and stretches northwards for several hundreds of miles, throwing off spurs east and west— being the backbone of the country—is of palæozoic origin; but the rocks of which it is formed being unfossiliferous, their exact position in point of age is undetermined. Fossils have been obtained in strata near Ardrossan, on Northern Yorke's Peninsula, which prove the rocks to be the equivalent of the silurian formation; it would, therefore, scarcely be hazarding too much to infer that the whole system of our primary stratified rocks is of the same age.

The palæozoic rocks of the colony are immediately succeeded by an immense area of tertiary limestone, abundantly fossiliferous, stretching eastwards to Victoria and westwards to Western Australia. It would seem as if nearly the whole of this part of Australia had for a lengthened period been submerged in a sea, the life of which was analagous to that now existing in the Indian and China Seas, and that only the summits of the highest hills in the chain already mentioned had peered above the waters, as so many little islands; thus indicating a division of Australia into two equal parts by a tropical sea running north and south. The carboniferous series have not been found, nor have rocks of oolitic origin. Igneous rocks occur in many parts, and volcanic rocks are well developed in the district of Mount Gambier. Auriferous drifts, of tertiary age, are dispersed in some localities, but gold has not hitherto been obtained anywhere in sufficient quantity to attract a large digging population. The colony is remarkably rich in copper and iron.

### 8.—Flora.

The flora of South Australia, as far as known, is less numerous in genera and species of plants than that of the other provinces of Australia; and, in spite of the large area of the colony, there is but little diversity in vegetation. In character, the South Australian flora is intermediate between the south-eastern, the south-western, and the tropical floras of Australia. The predominant orders are the leguminosæ, myrtaceæ, compositæ, proteaceæ, cruciferæ, rubiaceæ, and gramineæ. Both genera and species are singularly circumscribed in area, the rapid succession of forms and the contrast between those of the northern and southern parts of the colony being remarkable.

The bark of most of the trees is smooth and of a greyish color, owing to the slightness of the atmospheric changes. The leaves are, for the most part, coriaceous, rigid, pungent—of a shining glaucous color, and with a thick external coating as if to resist the heat, and retain the moisture. The flowers are generally bright-colored, yellow prevailing, and their vegetable fibre is fine. As in other parts of the continent, the eucalyptus and acacia genera prevail: thirty species only of eucalypti, and seventy of acacia, are known as yet within the limits of the colony. Plants abounding in essential and inflammable oils are frequent, but indigenous eatable fruits and root-bearing plants rare. There are a few poisonous plants—notably the *Lotus Australis.*

### 9.—*Character of Lands.*

Special and peculiar forms of plants are found in different regions—which may be called the regions of the forest land, scrub land, grass land, and the intertropical region.

The region of the forest land lies chiefly on the mountainous districts. The predominant forest trees are eucalypti, stringybark forming often whole forests in some mountainous districts, though it is seldom seen in the plains. The deep gullies are thickly covered with shrubs and ferns, and

the level tablelands with grass. The soil of these
tablelands is, generally speaking, very rich, and produces abundant crops of cereals, while that in the
gullies is mostly formed of black or sandy peat.
In such gullies all kinds of vegetables and European
fruits grow to perfection.

The regions of the so-called scrub lands occupy
a large portion of the whole area of the colony,
forming long stretches of arid plains. The soil
changes from loamy clay to sand, and the surface is
sometimes covered with fragments of silicious rocks,
ferruginous sand, and ironstone. Surface waters are
rare in this description of country; the vegetation is
consequently stunted, grasses and other herbage thinly
covering the ground where scrubs are growing. There
is an almost endless variety of shrubs, which are
interspersed with various trees. The leaves of the
scrub are usually of a glaucous green, and its appearance—except in the flowering season, when much
beauty clothes its surface—is somewhat monotonous.
Amongt the scrub plants is the saltbush (*atriplex
nummularia*), excellent feed for sheep.

The pasture lands, forming the principal part of
the area of the colony, consist of almost endless
undulating plains, stretching from the coast towards
the north and east. Near the coast the lands, of a
primary grassy character, are mostly under cultivation,
the soil varying in quality. In the interior, however,
these plains are so extensive as to be lost in the

horizon. Their surface is often saline, covered with sharp, angular, or weatherworn fragments of various sizes of ironstone, quartz, sandstone, and conglomerate, and supporting salt along with a scanty herbage of perennial grasses, cotton, sage, native peach, and other bushes constituting excellent fodder for live stock. During the summer season the more grassy lands have a sunburnt yellow appearance ; but directly the rainy season sets in they become suddenly of a deep rich green, and are soon clothed with luxuriant verdure and flowering plants. This season lasts from May till November. Here and there are large tracts of grass land called " Bay of Biscay." They have a peculiar undulating surface, but the dark chocolate-colored soil under them is good and produces fine wheat crops. The sea-beach is mostly bordered with a belt of arborescent shrubs and small trees of ramified growth.

The country near the northern coast of the intra-tropical region of the province consists principally of a tableland of from 60 to 150 feet above the level of the sea. It falls thence gently towards the ocean, although forming here and there into cliffs, which are fringed with dense thickets of various sized timber, matted together with bamboo and a variety of climbing plants and shrubs. The low lands near the sea are covered with dense mangroves. Grass grows luxuriantly nearly everywhere ; the soil is mostly good and of a dark brown color, with small nodules of ferruginous sandstone upon the surface.

## 10.—Naturalised Plants.

A number of grasses from other countries, and especially from Europe, have been introduced into South Australia, and have greatly improved the pasture. Besides these, the Scotch thistle, the cockspur, the Cape dandelion, the Bathurst burr, the French fly, the stink-aster, the sheepweed, and other troublesome weeds have obtained admission. The cereals and fruits of Europe have also generally thriven here. A description of these will be found further on under " Horticulture and Agriculture."

## 11.—Fauna.

The fauna of Australia is peculiarly rich in marsupials. Over 40 species are found in this province, as well as some 30 other species of small mammals. The existing marsupials are of moderate size, the largest not exceeding 200lbs. in weight; but remains of their predecessors, equal in size to the rhinoceros, have been discovered in the pleistocene formation. The most peculiar of the Australian animals are the duck-billed platypus and the spiny ant-eater. Of the placental series, the curious water-rats or beaver-rats deserve mention as being purely Australian. The dog, or dingo, is supposed to have been introduced.

The fish on the coasts are as yet imperfectly known; but the Avi Fauna is considerable—nearly 700 species are found in Australia. Amongst the most remarkable and beautiful birds are the parrots—of which

B

over 60 species exist — the bower-building birds,
mound-raising megapodes, and the emu. Game
species abound, and every bay along the coast
swarms with wild-fowl.

### 12.—Climate.

With the exception of the northern coast, which
is tropical, the climate of the whole colony is of an
unusually equal character, resembling that of the
southern parts of Europe. Towards the centre of
the continent there is less rain and a more per-
sistent heat than in Adelaide, but the general
character of the climate is similar. The clearness
and dryness of the atmosphere are extraordinary, and
happily weaken the effect of the periods of extreme
heat to which the province is subjected from time to
time during the summer months (December to March),
so that the thermometer is no true measure of the
degree in which our comforts are affected by the heat.
After March the temperature falls rapidly. April,
May, September, October, and November, enjoy an
almost ideal climate. From the end of May till the
beginning of September the weather is very similar
to that in England during April and May.

The mean temperature at the Adelaide Observatory
is 63° Fahrenheit, the maximum registered being
116°, and the minimum 32°; but in the hilly districts close to Adelaide, and in the south-east, the
temperature is several degrees lower.

In Adelaide the mean annual rainfall is about 21 inches, the greatest during a single year being 31, and the least 13. In the summer the average rainfall is less than an inch per month, and even in winter the rain is rarely continuous, and bright sunny days are the rule rather than the exception. In the hilly districts the mean annual rainfall is about 30 inches, and in the south-eastern counties it is also much greater than in Adelaide.

# Chap. II.—History.

## 1.—The Aborigines.

There is but scanty evidence as to the length of man's existence in Australia, as neither weapons nor implements have yet been found with the remains of fossil animals. Stone weapons are still used by many tribes, and the primitive art of splitting, grinding, and shaping rocks into hatchets and spear-heads is not yet lost.

As far as is known, the aborigines were never very numerous, and of late years their numbers have been much diminished by internecine quarrels, infanticide, diseases, and, above all, by their indiscretion when subjecting themselves to the habits, food, and clothing of Europeans. Many tribes have become wholly extinct, and the total known indigenous population of the colony, according to a census taken in 1876, was under 4,000, of whom only a thousand remain in the settled districts. Of nomadic habits, they live by the chase, by fishing, and on the roots of plants, neither cultivating the soil nor erecting fixed abodes. Although cunning and treacherous, their general disposition is peaceful, and they show considerable intelligence in adapting themselves to their special habits of life. Attempts have been made to better

their condition by the establishment of homes for
the adults and training-schools for the children; but
they can rarely be depended upon to remain long at
any settled employment, and show a marked objection
to dwell within closed walls.

The best known tribes are the Narrinyeri, the
Adelaides (extinct), the Encounter Bays, the Port
Lincolns, the Dieyeries, and the Woolnahs (Northern
Territory), all speaking different dialects. Their
language is musical, abounding in vowels and liquids.
Although they have many peculiar characteristics,
there seems to be a ground for thinking that the
Australians are remotely allied to the Papuans.
Although black in the skin, they have nothing of the
negro type; their hair is curly, but not woolly, and
grows abundantly on the face. The men are, as a
rule, well formed, and the women have also by nature
a good physique, but the life of complete drudgery
they undergo at the hands of their lords and masters
soon ages them. The chief weapons in use are
spears, throwing-sticks, waddies, boomerangs, and
shields of bark, and most tribes show some cleverness
in making nets and baskets of grass or fibre. As
compared with other races of savages, the accom-
plishments of the Australian are few; but it must be
remembered that the character of the climate and
abundance of the food they require are such that very
little call has existed on their ingenuity in supplying
the first necessaries of life. In spite of the persevering

attempts of benevolent persons, it would seem as if
the extinction of the aboriginal race is but a question
of time. [For further information on the aboriginal races, see "The Native Tribes of South
Australia," and "Folklore of the Aborigines," both
lying on the table in the Court.]

## 2.—Early Explorations.

Although Lieutenant Grant, of H.M.S. *Lady
Nelson*, sighted Cape Northumberland, Mount
Gambier, and Mount Schank as early as 1800, the
first person to acquire any knowledge of the coast
within the boundaries of the existing colony was
Captain Flinders, of the *Investigator*, who, in 1802,
explored the whole of the southern coast-line, naming
many of its principal features. The result of his
voyage does not seem to have tempted further examination till 1830, when Captain Sturt, with great
daring and judgment, worked his way from the Murrumbidgee to the Murray, and traced the latter river
through New South Wales and South Australia to its
mouth in Encounter Bay.

## 3.—Colonization.

The settlement of South Australia as a distinct
colony originated with a few gentlemen in London,
who, in 1831—the year after and consequent upon
Captain Sturt's explorations—made an application to
the Imperial Government for a charter to colonize a

portion of the land forming the present province. The application was unfavorably received, and the project remained in abeyance till 1834, when a meeting was held in Exeter Hall to discuss the principles of the scheme, propounded by Mr. E. Gibbon Wakefield, on which the new colony was to be established. The chief of these were that the land should in all cases be sold at a somewhat high price, that the blocks so purchased should not be larger than the buyers could easily cultivate, and that the revenue derived from the sale of lands should be applied to the importation of labor. On this basis an Act was passed through Parliament in 1834, which further contained the important principles—1st, that the colony should not be a charge upon the mother country; 2nd, that she should be free from any State church; 3rd, that no convicts should be transported into her territory. The terms of this charter are still maintained.

Commissioners were appointed to give effect to the Act, but before the colony could be established a certain quantity of land had to be sold. There was a great difficulty in finding purchasers, and the scheme nearly fell through; but at this critical juncture Mr. G. F. Angas promoted the South Australian Company, which bought sufficient land at twelve shillings an acre. Early in 1836 several vessels with colonists were laid on, and a survey party, under Colonel Light, was dispatched to explore

a site for the capital. On December 28, 1836, the
first Governor (Captain Hindmarsh) landed on the
shores of Holdfast Bay, and proclaimed the foundation of the colony.

The boundaries at this time were comprised between
132° and 141° E. long., and between the Southern
Ocean and 26° S. lat.; but in 1861 a tract of country,
known as "No Man's Land," was added, making
129° E. the western boundary, and in 1863, when the
colony determined to lay down the trans-continental
telegraph, another addition was made, consisting of
the country stretching northward to the Indian Ocean.

### 4.—Government.

The Government of the colony was originally in
the hands of a Board of Commissioners, three of
whom were resident in London and one in Adelaide;
but from the time of Captain Hindmarsh's arrival the
executive power rested with the Governor and a
Council of eight members—four official and four
nominee. In 1851, however, a constitution was
granted, by which a Legislative Council, two-thirds
of whose members were elected by the people, was
authorised. The colonists soon began to agitate for
Responsible Government, which was granted them by
the existing Constitution Act passed in 1856. By
this Act the government is vested in a Governor and
two Houses of Parliament, called respectively the
Legislative Council and the House of Assembly.

The Legislative Council, which cannot be dissolved
by the Governor, is elected by ballot, the whole
province forming one electoral district for the purpose.
There are eighteen members, six of whom retire every
fourth year. The electorate is based on a small
property qualification.

The House of Assembly, which is liable to dissolu-
tion by the Governor, is elected for three years, the
province being divided into twenty-two electoral
districts, returning altogether forty-six members,
whose services are gratuitous. The electorate is based
on manhood suffrage.*

Responsible Government is carried on by six
Ministers, members of the Legislature, who form the
Cabinet, and are *ex officio* members of the Executive
Council, advising the Crown in the person of Her
Majesty's representative, the Governor. Each Minister
has control of several departments of the public
service, the duties of which are conducted by per-
manent official heads.

All the affairs of the colony are thus under the
control of the two Houses of Parliament. Each
House is vested with equal powers, with the exception
that the Legislative Council cannot initiate financial
measures. The Crown retains power to disallow
bills opposed to the principles of Imperial legislation.

* NOTE.—The number of electoral districts was originally eighteen, returning
thirty-six members, but in 1873 the number of districts was increased to
twenty-two, and members to forty-six.

The two Houses model their proceedings in accordance with the practice of the House of Commons.

### 5.—*Local Government.*

Local self-government was established as far back as 1840, when the Corporation of Adelaide was formed, and has now become general throughout the province. In twenty-one towns it presents itself under the form of municipal corporations, managed by members elected at stated periods by ratepayers, and invested with extensive powers under a special Act. In the country one hundred and twelve bodies, styled District Councils, elected by ratepayers living within the limits of a proclaimed district, have control over the affairs of their district, the State supplementing pound for pound all sums raised and expended on public works.

### 6.—*Population.*

The population exceeds a quarter of a million, of whom the majority are resident in the country districts, and employed directly or indirectly in the cultivation of the soil, or in the production of mineral and pastoral wealth. The native-born element already forms 60 per cent., and the proportion of males to females is but slightly in favor of the former. The marriage rate has been steadily increasing during the last ten years. The proportion per 1,000 of the population of marriages in 1879 was $8\frac{3}{4}$; of births, $38\frac{3}{4}$; of deaths, 14. The births numbered 9,902 ; the marriages 2,238; and the deaths 3,580.   It is a noteworthy fact that the increase of population within the last few years has been greater than at any previous period.

### 7.—Centres of Population.

The capital city is Adelaide, with a population of nearly 40,000, exclusive of the suburbs, which furnish about 25,000 more.   Adelaide contains over 8,500 buildings and seventy-eight miles of made streets.   The annual rateable value of property, excluding Government offices, churches, and other public institutions, is £354,000, and the total value was computed last year at from eight to nine millions sterling.   The town is well supplied with water from the Mount Lofty range of hills, at the foot of which it lies, and the distance from the sea is seven miles only.   The chief shipping place of the colony is Port Adelaide, connected by rail with the metropolis.   The largest provincial towns, exclusive of Port Adelaide and the suburbs of Adelaide, are the Burra, Mount Gambier, Wallaroo, Glenelg, Kapunda, and Gawler.

NOTE.—Adelaide lies in latitude 37° 57′ S. and longitude 138° 38′ E., and is about five miles distant from the eastern shores of Gulf St. Vincent ; and Port Adelaide, the principal seaport, is distant about seven miles from the capital, with which it is connected by railway.

### 8.—South Australian Explorations.

The first explorers were adventurous persons in charge of live stock, travelling to the colony from New

South Wales and Victoria; illustrious amongst whom, and still resident in the colony, are Messrs. Charles Bonney and George Hamilton. Their enterprises were soon followed, within narrower limits, from Adelaide as a centre, by colonists in search of pasture lands. Great hardships were often endured by these, and not unfrequently valuable lives sacrificed in the search. The natives occasionally resented what they not unnaturally regarded as an unwarrantable intrusion on their territory; and want of water was an enemy even more deadly.

One of the first and bravest explorers from Adelaide was Mr. E. J. Eyre, who subsequently became Governor of Jamaica. In 1840 Mr. Eyre undertook the leadership of a party to explore the unknown country lying between Adelaide and King George's Sound, and after losing all his companions, with the exception of one black boy, reached his destination in great distress.

The next explorer of note was Captain Sturt, who, in 1844, attempted to find the inland sea, at that time supposed to occupy the centre of the continent; and after incredible suffering during eighteen months he returned to Adelaide, having discovered Cooper's Creek.

Several expeditions were undertaken by the Government and private individuals between 1857 and 1859, without adding much to the knowledge of the interior; but in 1859 Mr. Stuart, Sturt's former companion and draughtsman, commenced that grand series of explorations which, after many difficulties and disappointments, terminated successfully in July, 1862, by the crossing of the continent from the Southern to the Indian Ocean.

In 1862, Mr. John McKinlay, sent in search of Burke and Wills, made a dash across the continent with great dispatch and success. It is recorded of him that "for cool perseverance and kind considera-"tion for his followers, for modesty and quiet daring, "Mr McKinlay was unequalled as an explorer."

In 1872 Colonel Warburton, with the true courage of a British officer, gallantly effected his remarkable expedition from the centre across the western interior of Australia, reaching the River De Grey in an exhausted state, after enduring many hardships. This expedition is noteworthy as having been performed exclusively by the use of camels, which were kindly supplied by Sir Thomas Elder.

In 1874 Mr. John Forrest, a Western Australian, travelled from King George's Sound to Adelaide north of the route which Eyre had travelled thirty years before. Amongst other explorers are Mr. Gosse, Mr. Ernest Giles, and Mr. Lewis, who have made valuable discoveries in various directions in the interior of the country, and have added considerably to our knowledge. The most recent exploration is that of Mr. Alexander Forrest, brother to Mr. John Forrest, who, in 1879, started from the De Grey River for Port Darwin; but, put aside by the rugged character of the country north of him, diverged eastward up the Fitzroy River and struck into the overland telegraph line at Charlotte Waters.

## 9.—Immigration.

A steady and moderate increase of population suitable to the requirements of the country is and will be, for many years to come, essential to the welfare and advancement of the province. Such additional labor is readily absorbed without producing any disturbance of the labor market. In accordance with the principles on which the colony was founded, immigration has for many years been paid for out of the money derived from the sale of lands. Although free immigration is now temporarily discontinued, assisted passages are given to agricultural, and other laborers, artisans, domestic servants, and other desirable colonists, on the nomination of friends already in the colony. Land order warrants to the value of £20 are granted, to persons who pay their own passages, by the Agent-General for South Australia, 8, Victoria Chambers, Westminster, London, from whom full information respecting immigration can be procured.

# ADELAIDE
## SOUTH AUSTRALIA
### DIAGRAM SHOWING

POPULATION  ACRES SOLD  ACRES CULTIVATED
ACRES IN WHEAT & WHEAT HARVESTED

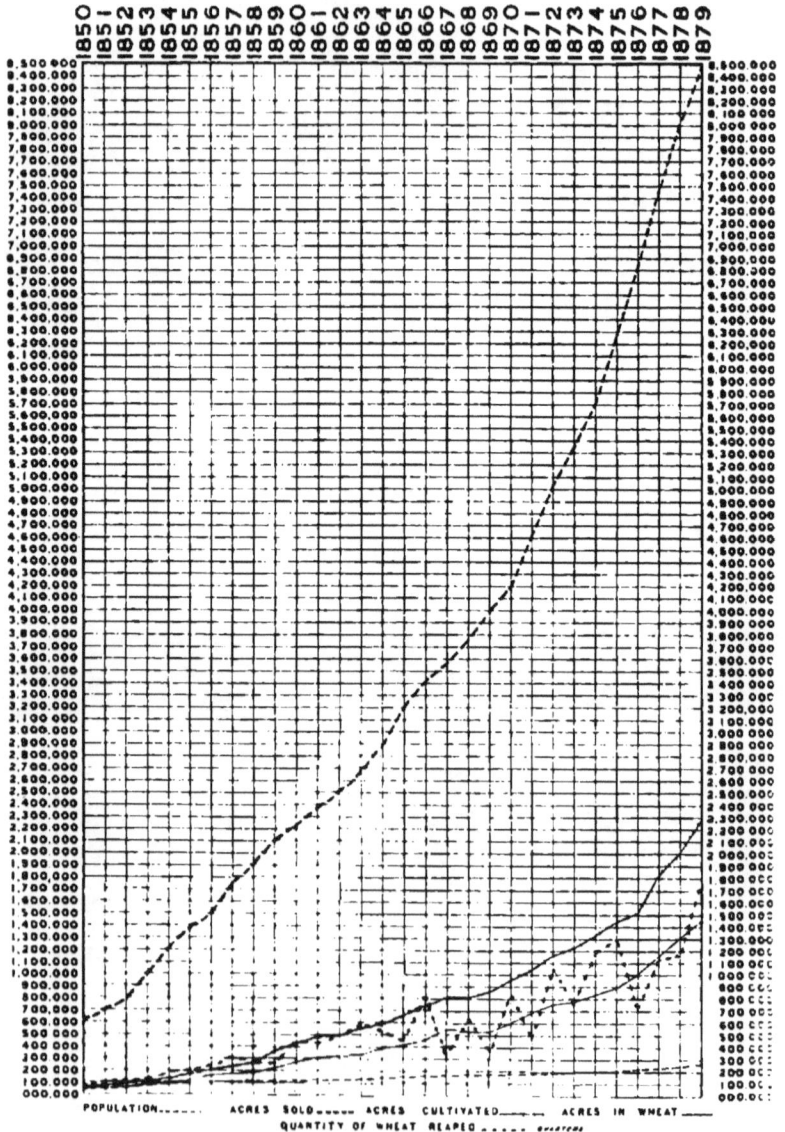

1850 1851 1852 1853 1854 1855 1856 1857 1858 1859 1860 1861 1862 1863 1864 1865 1866 1867 1868 1869 1870 1871 1872 1873 1874 1875 1876 1877 1878 1879

POPULATION........  ACRES SOLD_____  ACRES CULTIVATED_____  ACRES IN WHEAT ____
QUANTITY OF WHEAT REAPED ...... ........

SURVEYOR GENERAL'S OFFICE, ADELAIDE. *Fraser S. Crawford, Photo-lithographer*

# Chap. III.—The Land.

## 1.—Its Occupation.

At a rough estimate, about 250,000 square miles of country are at present put to more or less profitable use. Agriculture has not extended 100 miles from the southern coast, and pastoral occupation cannot be said to have reached further than 500 miles, though lately squatters have taken up large areas of land in the centre of the continent, discovered by recent explorations. Over five and a quarter million acres of land had been sold completely at the end of 1879, and there were besides at that date over 3,000,000 acres held upon credit, the greater proportion of which will in due course pass absolutely to the purchasers. About one in every four acres of the land sold is under tillage; the remainder is used for sheep and cattle.

## 2.—The Land Laws.

Long leases at small rentals are offered to capitalists willing to occupy waste lands, but it is only upon condition that the Government may resume their lands, after paying due compensation for improvements made by the lessee, at from twelve to thirty-six months' notice. There are also special provisions for the sale of township, suburban, and the poorer or scrub lands; but the great aim of the existing land laws is

to promote agricultural settlement and improvement,
and to give the *bonâ fide* farmer with but small capital
the preference of all the lands offered for sale.

The chief principles embodied by the land laws are
purchase *after* survey by Government ; deferred pay-
ments ; limitation of area held upon credit to
1,000 acres of ordinary lands or 640 acres of lands
reclaimed by drainage ; conditions of improvement
and cultivation ; and, as far as possible, compulsory
residence. The land is sold by auction in blocks
varying in size from sixty to 1,000 acres, a large
quantity being put up on one day. The upset price
is £1 an acre.

### 3.—Land Transfer.

Dealings in landed property are much facilitated by
the Real Property Act, originated by Sir R. R. Torrens,
which provides that the title to all lands alienated
from the Crown since 1858, when the Act came into
force, shall depend upon registration. Land acquired
before that date may be brought under the Act, upon
application, subject to a certain amount of protection
to equities which may arise. The total value of the
lands brought under this law amounts to nearly twelve
millions sterling.

### 4.—Pastoral Settlement.

The pastoral lessees—more commonly called *squatters*—have, from the earliest days, been the pioneers

of settlement; and, notwithstanding the large area
of land sold to agriculturists during the last few
years, the acreage taken up for squatting purposes,
and the number of flocks and herds have considerably
increased. The squatter, who, by the advance of
agricultural settlement, has been driven from the lands
near the seacoast, has found a refuge in the district
before alluded to as the "Far North," and a few
adventurous men have removed their flocks and herds
towards the centre of the continent. Greater attention
has been paid of late to the enclosure of sheep runs,
the formation of dams and reservoirs, and the sinking
of wells, and an improved quality both of stock and
wool has resulted. Moreover, large numbers of sheep
are now owned by agriculturists, who advantageously
combine sheep-farming with the cultivation of the soil.

Some conception of the growth of the pastoral
interest during the last ten years may be formed from
the following facts:—

|  | 1869. | 1874. | 1879. |
|---|---|---|---|
| Total area of land (sq. miles) leased from the Crown for pastoral purposes .. .. | 58,000 | 89,000 | 177,000 |
| No. of horses in the colony | 73,828 | 93,122 | 130,052 |
| No. of horned cattle      " | 119,697 | 185,342 | 266,217 |
| No. of sheep              " | 4,436,955 | 6,120,211 | 6,140,396 |
| No. of pigs               " | 63,826 | 78,019 | 90,548 |
| No. of goats              " | 13,977 | 16,907 | 11,277 |

C

The favorite kind of sheep in the interior is the merino, but on the coast long-wools are preferred by many. The cattle are frequently of excellent breed, including Durham, Hereford, Devons, Alderneys, and Scotch long-hairs, of which good pedigree stocks have been introduced. There are one or two flocks of Angora goats, but no great progress has been made in the rearing of these animals. Sir Thomas Elder introduced camels in 1866. Their numbers have greatly increased, and they are proving a valuable acquisition.

### 5.—Wool.

If the wind and tendon of the horse, or the firmness and delicacy of the flesh of horned cattle, gain when reared on the natural fodder of a warm and sunny climate, tempered by tree shade and camping grounds which afford shelter from extremes of weather, so the character of wool is affected by the nature of the country the sheep depasture. Two distinct classes of fodder influence the wool of South Australia: that of the grassy or coast, and the salt-bush or interior country. In each class there is a subdivision into hill or plain feed. Thus many characters of wool are produced from the two chief breeds of sheep adopted by the colonists. Of high-class Merino, the Mount Crawford, Canowie, Levels, Keyneton, and Terlinga stand prominent. Of Lincoln, the Collingrove and Moorak; and the wool of both breeds, where carefully tended, acquires special degrees of strength and lustre. Also, whilst the grassy country will produce the finest, softest, and densest fleece, the remarkable freedom from all disease and larger development of carcase in the saltbush country causes the quantity and length of wool of the sheep fed there to well compensate for a relative harshness and coarseness.

## 6.—Agriculture.

That the general character of the land, so far as it has been tested, is in a high degree favorable to agricultural settlement, may be judged from the fact that nearly half of the male population of the community are engaged in farming pursuits—chiefly cereal. The settled land may be divided into three classes—the plains, which for the most part are at once available for the plough; the hilly country, where more or less clearing of timber must be done to render the land fit for cultivation; and scrub lands, which in some cases are of inferior quality, but in others are only kept from being cultivated owing to the expense and labor that would be involved in removing the timber. A fourth class might be added, consisting of comparatively level country, sprinkled with sheaoak and other small timber, which can be removed at a comparatively small cost.

Notwithstanding the dryness of the climate the soil is productive, and consequent on that dryness the quality of the products is excellent. Not only do English fruits, vegetables, and cereals of all kinds grow to perfection, but many semi-tropical products do well, the earth yielding a bountiful return for a moderate amount of labor. The system of farming is, as a rule, simple. There is little or no exertion made to return to the soil the ingredients which are taken from it by the process of vegetable growth. The land is either cropped year after year, for the most part with wheat, until it becomes thoroughly exhausted, or it is treated to alternate fallow ; but, doubtless, as settlement spreads, and the quantity of cultivable virgin soil diminishes and population increases, a change will take place in this respect.

## 7.—Wheat.

Of the total area under cultivation (2,271,058 acres) nearly two-thirds is cropped with wheat, of which nearly one and a-half million acres were reaped at the last harvest, December, 1879, yielding an aggregate of over fourteen million bushels. The progress made in wheat cultivation has of late years been very rapid, as may be gathered from the fact that in 1868 the area under wheat was only half a million acres, and that in 1875 it nearly reached 900,000 acres.

The actual production of wheat to the acre is small, averaging about 9½ bushels, but the cost of

PER BUSHEL / POUNDS

| Year | | EXPORTS | |
|---|---|---|---|
| 1870 | WHEAT | 8,370 | |
| | FLOUR | 27,370 | |
| | TONS | 35,740 | |
| 1871 | WHEAT | 56,670 | |
| | FLOUR | 46,760 | |
| | TONS | 103,430 | |
| 1872 | WHEAT | 26,628 | |
| | FLOUR | 34,738 | |
| | TONS | 61,367 | |
| 1873 | WHEAT | 58,114 | |
| | FLOUR | 103,543 | |
| | TONS | 161,657 | |
| 1874 | WHEAT | 42,353 | |
| | FLOUR | 58,000 | |
| | TONS | 100,353 | |
| 1875 | WHEAT | 100,129 | |
| | FLOUR | 76,209 | |
| | TONS | 176,338 | |
| 1876 | WHEAT | 148,465 | |
| | FLOUR | 65,000 | |
| | TONS | 213,465 | |
| 1877 | WHEAT | 25,500 | |
| | FLOUR | 67,500 | |
| | TONS | 93,000 | |
| 1878 | WHEAT | 93,438 | |
| | FLOUR | 62,276 | |
| | TONS | 155,714 | |
| 1879 | WHEAT | 104,688 | |
| | FLOUR | 70,518 | |
| | TONS | 175,706 | |

By. R.H.Lingen.

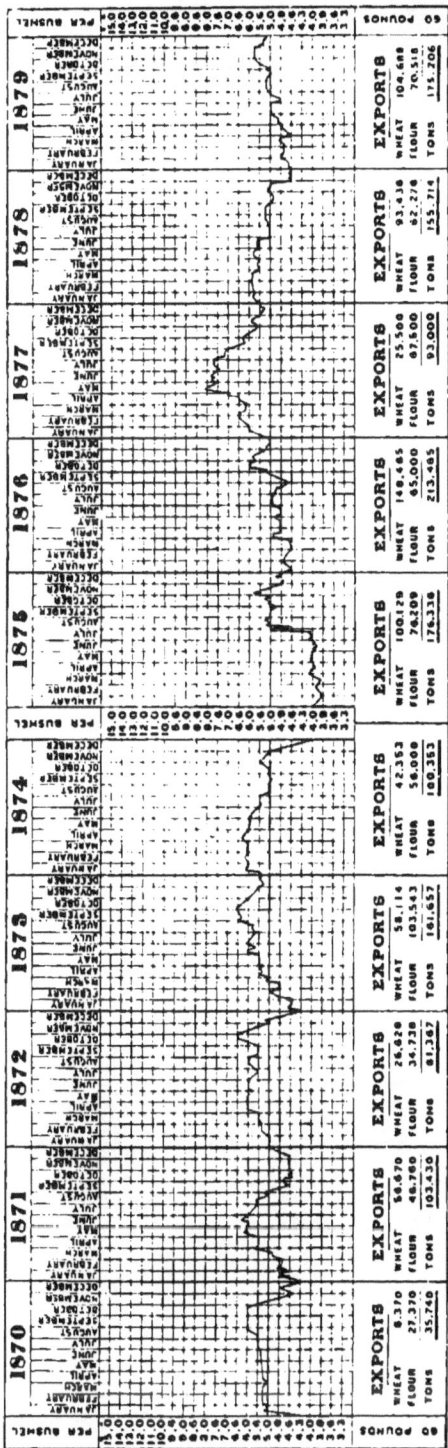

SURVEYOR GENERAL'S OFFICE, ADELAIDE  Frazer S Crawford, Photo lithographer

cultivation is also small. The farmer but lightly ploughs his ground. The seed is sown broadcast by machinery, at the rate of sixty to seventy acres per day; and by the machine known as Ridley's reaper—of South Australian invention—eight to ten acres can be reaped per day by a man with two horses. This reaper combs and threshes the grain out of the ear. It is then winnowed in the field and taken to market. The stalk is left standing ; sometimes to be fed over, and then burnt, and sometimes to be cut by the mowing-machine and chaffed for fodder. No system of rotation of crops has yet been arrived at, except in the South-Eastern Districts. The greater portion of the land has been sown with wheat continuously for many successive years without manure or rest, and has received a minimum of cultivation.

Of the quality of the South Australian wheat it is almost needless to write. It fetches the highest price in the London market, and has obtained the highest awards at every International Exhibition where it has been shown. To give some idea of the quantity of wheat produced, it is worth mentioning that after supplying her own wants the colony had over 300,000 tons of breadstuffs, valued at nearly two and three-quarter millions sterling, available for export last season ; and yet the season was but moderately prosperous.

## 8.—Wine.

The rich chocolate loam, and the ferruginous soil with lime, of the hillsides and plains in the neighbourhood of Adelaide, are admirably adapted for the production of wine grapes; and wine-growing has been carried on from the early days of the colony, when cuttings were obtained from some of the best stocks of the Cape of Good Hope, France, Germany, and Spain. Inexperience has naturally led to many failures; but of later years much greater care has been taken, both in adapting the soil and position of the vineyard to the grape, and in the manufacture of the wine. This has been followed by a considerable improvement in the quality of the wines produced, and there is now good reason to hope that they may become successful competitors in the European market. Most of the South Australian wines are of a full-bodied or sweet character; but on the hills lighter wines are readily made.

The extent of lands planted with vines in 1879 was over 4,000 acres, and the produce of the vintage of March, 1880, was nearly half a million gallons, or about 200 gallons per acre of vines grown for wine. The greater part of this wine is consumed in the colony; but in spite of obstructive fiscal laws, over £16,000 worth was exported in 1879 to Great Britain and the neighbouring colonies.

## 9.—Olives.

The dryness of the climate, the absence of frost,

and the length of the coast-line, give to a large area
of the colony unrivalled advantages for the cultivation
of the olive tree; and if it has not yet been carried
out on any very extensive scale, it is because colonists
are accustomed to turn over their capital so quickly
that they have not the patience required by the slow
growth of this tree. Many of the best varieties of
olives were introduced soon after the foundation of
the colony, and for years small quantities of oil of
excellent quality have been made. It is only during
the last three or four years, however, that this industry
has acquired any magnitude. Several thousand
gallons were made during the past season, and the
area under olives is considerable. The oil, when
made, commands a ready sale in the colony at a
higher price than the imported article.

## 10.—Minor Products.

Besides wheat, attention is bestowed upon the cultivation of hay, barley, rye, potatoes, field peas, lucerne,
and to a small extent of flax, hops, and artificial grasses.

The total yield of these products during the season
1879-80 was as follows:—

| | | | | | |
|---|---|---|---|---|---|
| Barley | .. | 202,000 bushels, | gathered from | 15,100 | acres. |
| Oats | .... | 61,000 " | " | " 4,100 | " |
| Peas | .... | 58,000 " | " | " 4,000 | " |
| Hay | .... | 296,000 tons | " | " 265,000 | " |
| Potatoes | .. | 27,000 " | " | over 7,000 | " |

Hops are grown with great success in the South-
Eastern District, and also in the Adelaide hills.

Flax is an indigenous plant, which thrives well, and, having the special merit of cleansing soils, will be a valuable production as soon as the means of harvesting are cheapened, and facilities for retting provided. Not only is flax useful as a fibre plant, but the linseed yields valuable oil and fodder.

Tobacco is also indigenous in many parts of the colony, but it is not yet cultivated for commercial purposes. Amongst other plants which have not yet got beyond the experimental stage of cultivation may be mentioned the castor-oil plant, the sunflower, mustard, rape, canary-seeds, lupin, maize, lentils, chicory, osier, broom, millet, esparto grass, opium, and many plants used in the distilling of perfumes.

Attempts have been made to establish sericulture as a colonial industry, but hitherto with no substantial results. The colony is already possessed of a good stock of the best varieties of silk-mulberries, and the tree thrives well. The climate appears to be admirably suited to the silkworm, and some excellent cocoons have been sent to International Exhibitions, and gained high commendation there.

## 11.—Horticulture.

Nearly all kinds of European fruits are produced to perfection in the colony—those of the Continent almost everywhere ; and the more peculiarly English fruits, such as the strawberry and raspberry, in the hilly districts. In good seasons many kinds of fruits—especially apricots, peaches, plums, and grapes —grow in great abundance. The earliest of the spring fruits is the loquat, which ripens before the end of September. Cherries and strawberries follow in October and November, and then gooseberries, currants, and raspberries. At Christmas time the first of the apricots and figs are ready for eating, and soon after peaches, plums, and grapes are ready, not only for home consumption, but for export, considerable quantities being sent to the neighboring colonies. Apples, pears, melons, nuts, filberts, walnuts, and Spanish chestnuts, and a variety of other fruits, carry on the supply till the orange season, which begins about June and lasts until November.

The sultana, muscatel, and other raisin-making vines are largely grown in the vineyards, and some eighty tons of raisins, equal to the best imported are manufactured every year. The Xante grape, from which currants are made, is also grown, and the currant-making industry, though still in its infancy, promises to be of great importance.

During the summer season a large quantity of jam is made, much of which is exported, more especially the apricot, peach, and plum varieties.

## 12.—Gold.

In South Australia gold-mining has hitherto made but little progress. Several small discoveries have been made from time to time at Echunga, Jupiter

Creek, in the Barossa Ranges, at Mount Pleasant, Waukaringa, and other places, and connected with it small diamonds have been found in the Echunga goldfields. There is continuously a small gold-digging population.

### 13.—Copper.

The only mineral which has as yet contributed materially to the prosperity of the colony is copper, of which over sixteen million pounds' (£16,000,000) worth have been exported since the discovery of the first mine at Kapunda in 1842. Several other valuable mines were subsequently discovered. The most famous are the Burra Burra, Wallaroo, and Moonta, the last two of which are still being worked.

Owing to the prevailing low prices, the copper-mining industry has not been very prosperous for the last three years, the export of copper and copper ore during 1879 having reached only £351,388; but there is no sign of failing in the existing mines, and north of Port Augusta lodes of copper ore can be traced for miles across the country. A railway is being constructed through this district, and as soon as the price of copper rises, mines will probably be worked there.

### 14.—Iron.

The deposits of iron in the province are of great richness and extent, but, owing to the absence and high price of coal they have been but little worked. Native iron has been found so pure that it has, without any preparation, been welded on to a piece of manufactured iron and stood well. An attempt was made about six years ago to smelt the iron ore with wood, and a few tons of first-class pig iron were produced; but owing to hitches at the first the undertaking was abandoned. Some of the veins discovered are as much as forty feet wide.

### 15.—Silver and Lead.

Lead ore is found in large quantities in several places, and generally contains a proportion of silver, in many instances as high as fifty or sixty ounces to the ton; but the cost of smelting has hitherto prevented the extraction of the metal. Silver ore yielding as high as 30 per cent. of silver has been found, and some rich ore is known to exist on private property.

### 16.—Other Minerals.

Bismuth has been found in several places, notably at Balhannah, from which mine zinc and cobalt have also been raised. Amongst other useful mineral productions found are:—Antimony, asbestos, baryta, bitumen, cobalt, calcspar, dolomite, fireclay, fluorspar, Fuller's earth, gypsum, kaolin clay, lignite, marble, magnesia, magnesian limestone, mica, ochre, platinum, salt, slate (very fine, both roofing and paving), soapstone, and native sulphur. Of these gypsum and slate are extracted in considerable quantities, and used commercially. In the South-East a remarkable substance called coorongite is found on the surface; it occurs in thin tough cakes, and a brilliant illuminating mineral oil has been obtained from it by distillation. A company has recently been formed to bore for this oil at Salt Creek.

# Chap. IV.—Public Works & Institutions.

## 1.—Cost.

Up to the end of December, 1879, a sum of about seven and a-half millions had been expended on public works out of loans specially raised for the purpose. Of this amount nearly four millions has been spent on railways, half a million on harbor improvements, three-quarters of a million on water-works, a little over half a million a-piece on telegraphs and main roads, nearly a quarter of a million on schoolhouses, a hundred and twenty thousand on jetties and lighthouses, and the balance for sundry other works. Beyond this, however, large sums taken out of the Land Fund and out of General Revenue have, from the earliest days, been disbursed upon roads, bridges, buildings, jetties, lighthouses, and other undertakings of a public nature.

## 2.—Railways.

With the exception of a few miles of suburban railroad, the Government has undertaken the construction and maintenance of all the railways in the province; and although at present they yield a mean return of only about $2\frac{3}{4}$ per cent. on their cost, the benefits of the consequent extension of the margin of cultivation are held to counterbalance the burthen of interest which falls on the general public.

Over 500 miles of public railroad were open to the public at the close of 1879. The standard gauge for the main trunk lines is 5ft. 3in.—the same as on the Victorian lines; but in the outlying districts, where speed is of little and cheapness of great importance, the 3ft. 6in. gauge has been adopted.

The average charge for conveying passengers may be estimated at about $1^1/_2$d. per mile, and for a ton of goods from 2d to 3d. per mile. A bushel of wheat is carried from the Burra to Port Adelaide, a distance of 100 miles, for 7d.; and the rates charged on all the lines are proportionately low.

Over 250 miles of railway are now in course of construction.

### 3.—Roads and Bridges.

From the earliest days the importance of opening up the country by means of good roads was fully recognised; and during the past years upwards of one and three-quarter millions have been devoted to these works, the whole cost of which, with the exception of £200,000, has been defrayed out of the General Revenue, no special toll or rate having been levied. Of the 3,300 miles of main roads open to the public at the end of 1879, about 1,300 are macadamized. All these roads are under the care of Local Main Road Boards; but in addition to these main lines perhaps as many more miles of district or by-roads have been constructed and are kept in repair by local municipalities. For this purpose funds are raised by a rate on landed property, supplemented by grants-in-aid from the General Revenue.

The colony can boast of several fine bridges. The most notable is that at Edward's Crossing, over the River Murray, which is 190 feet long, and cost £125,000 to build. The next bridge in importance is the Jervois Bridge, over the stream at Port Adelaide. There are also several handsome bridges over the Torrens in Adelaide, and many substantial structures across the rivers and creeks in country districts.

*4.—Waterworks, Drainage, and Lighthouses.*

The supply of water was first undertaken by Government in 1857. In addition to a high-pressure supply from the River Torrens to the city and suburbs of Adelaide, water has been laid on to several centres of population, among which are Port Adelaide, Glenelg, Port Augusta, Port Pirie, Port Elliot, Kadina, Moonta, and Kapunda.

At present the drainage of Adelaide is defective; but a scheme of deep drainage, submitted by the late Mr. W. Clark, C.E., is being carried out under the supervision of Mr. Oswald Brown, C.E.

On thirteen prominent points on the southern coast lighthouses have been erected; and as there is a complete system of marine survey, wrecks are not frequent.

## 5.—*Postal Communication.*

Considering how thinly populated and extensive the outlying settled districts are, more than ordinary postal facilities are afforded to the public. Direct communication with Europe is maintained by two lines of packets, each of which dispatch steamers twice a month. There is a daily overland mail to Victoria and New South Wales, besides ship mails about twice a week. The average number of mails sent away daily from Adelaide is 326. Money-order offices are established in connection with most of the Post Offices, and money can also be sent by telegraph.

A uniform rate of twopence per half ounce is charged upon inland and intercolonial letters; and newspapers are forwarded free of charge to any part of the world.

## 6.—*Telegraphs.*

At the end of 1879 there were 4,400 miles of telegraph lines, and 6,000 of wire open to the public. Every township of any importance is connected with the capital by wire, the number of stations open being 150—between which telegrams are sent at a uniform rate of a shilling for ten words.

To South Australia belongs the honor of having, at her sole cost and unaided by the sister colonies, constructed the trans-continental line, which joins the Indian and the Southern Oceans, and brings Australia into continuous communication with Europe and the rest of the civilized world. This line is over 2,000 miles long, and was carried across a previously quite unknown country for the greater part of that distance.

## 7.—Administration of Justice.

The legal tribunals consist of a Supreme Court, with three Judges, and a Court of Insolvency in Adelaide, and Local Courts of civil jurisdiction in all the principal towns and townships. The Judges hold Circuit Courts at Naracoorte and Mount Gambier twice a year. Police Courts have also been established in Adelaide, and a few other towns, to deal summarily with offences against the peace, larcenies, and other minor criminal offences, and to commit to the Supreme Court.

The Supreme Court enjoys all the powers of the Courts of Queen's Bench, Common Pleas, and Exchequer, and fulfils the functions of the Courts of Chancery and of Vice-Admiralty. It also grants probates and letters of administration, and hears appeals from all the tribunals of inferior jurisdiction.

The Local Courts of Full Jurisdiction can adjudicate in all personal actions in amounts up to £100, and in actions of ejectment where the land is under the Real Property Act, and does not exceed £100 in value. Local Courts of Limited Jurisdiction can only decide suits involving claims under £20 in value. In the former case, the Court consists of a Special

D

Magistrate, two Justices of the Peace, or a Jury of four; in the latter, of a Special Magistrate alone, or of two Justices of the Peace alone.

The Insolvency Court is presided over by a Commissioner (who is also the Special Magistrate of the Adelaide Local Court), who has power to grant first, second, and third class certificates, the last of which does not operate as a discharge from debt; and to order imprisonment for a term not exceeding three years in cases of fraudulent insolvency.

Inquests are conducted by the Magistrates in the country districts; but a Coroner presides over all inquests held in the city and suburbs.

There is an efficient Police Force, consisting of detectives and mounted and foot constables, comprising about 300 men.

## 8.—Education.

The administration of the public schools is in the hands of a Responsible Minister, and the object of the existing Act is to educate every child in the colony up to a certain standard. The system is practically secular, but not to the exclusion of Bible-reading. All children between seven and thirteen years of age are obliged to attend school not less than thirty-five days in each quarter of a year. The only compulsory subjects are reading, writing, and arithmetic; but instruction is also given in other branches. The ordinary fee for primary schools is 4d. per week for children under eight years of age, and 6d. for older children, but gratuitous instruction is provided for children whose parents are unable to afford payment.

The number of primary schools in operation during 1879 was 220; that of children in attendance at these being 30,000. In country districts, where Government schools have not been built, provisional schools are established. Besides these schools there are seventy evening schools in operation. The number of teachers is nearly 800, of whom more than half are females.

In addition to the State schools there are nearly 300 private schools, including several of the grammar school type. The State does not undertake secondary education, with the exception of having an advanced school for girls and a training college for teachers.

Higher education is provided for by a University founded in 1872, and supported partly by private munificence and partly by Government.

Amongst the most useful institutions of an educational character are the Adelaide Botanic Garden and the South Australian Institute, containing under one roof a public and circulating library, a museum, and reading-room in Adelaide, and with branches in the country districts.

## 9.—Religion.

The colony was founded upon principles entirely opposed to any connection between Church and State.

The beneficial results of this freedom of religion from
State assistance and control may be estimated from
the fact that two-thirds of the population—scattered
though it be—have provided themselves with suitable
accommodation for the observance of public worship.
The number of churches and other buildings thus
used is over 900, and the total number of sittings
about 150,000.

The Church of England stands numerically at the
head of the denominations, but the Wesleyan Methodists have the largest number of churches. The
Roman Catholics, Lutherans, Presbyterians, Baptists,
Primitive Methodists, Congregationalists, and Bible
Christians have (in order) from 28,000 to 7,500 ad-
herents; and there are a number of other smaller sects.
Excluding those cases in which objection was taken
to affording the information, about 85 per cent. of the
whole population are members of Protestant Churches,
and the remaining 15 per cent. Roman Catholics.

An efficient system of Sunday schools is spread
throughout the colony, and they are attended by
about 40,000 children.

## 10.—Charitable Institutions.

Ample provision is made in public, semi-private,
and private institutions for the relief of the helpless
section of the community. There are hospitals for
the sick, asylums for orphans and neglected children,
for the poor and infirm, for the deaf and dumb and

blind, and for the insane; a retreat for sailors, a club
for bushmen, a children's hospital, an inebriate retreat,
and mission stations for the natives, and other
charities.

## 11.—Local Defences.

It is only within the last few years that a system
of military defence has been introduced. Well-
armed forts have been erected to cover the approach
to Port Adelaide, and a military road is being made
at the rear of the sandhills skirting the eastern coast
of St. Vincent's Gulf. The defence force consists of
volunteers of over 1,000 men, comprising two batteries
of artillery, one troop of cavalry, and nine companies
of infantry. A first-class band of forty performers is
attached to this force. There is also a body of rifle
volunteers of over 500 men.

# Chap. V.—Commerce and Manufactures.

## 1.—*Imports and Exports.*

The annexed table of imports and exports reveals the rapid development of commercial relations.

In 1838 the value of the exports did not exceed £5,000; in 1869 it amounted to nearly £3,000,000; by 1876 it had advanced to considerably over five and a quarter millions (£5,355,021), or £22 0s. 3d. per head of the population; but in 1879, owing to the reduced value of produce, the amount fell to four and three-quarter millions (£4,762,727), or £19 15s. per head of the population.

The imports, which in a measure represent the payment for the exports, have augmented concurrently with them. In 1838 the value of the imports was under £160,000; in 1869 it had increased to two and three-quarter millions; and in 1879 it reached five millions (£5,014,149), or about £19 18s. per head of the population.

## 2.—*Nature of Exports.*

1. Breadstuffs have for many years occupied a foremost place amongst the staple products of the province. During the last five years the most valuable export was that of 1876, which amounted to nearly

# ADELAIDE

## SOUTH AUSTRALIA

## DIAGRAM SHOWING

POPULATION  SHIPPING      EXPORTS   IMPORTS

& COMBINED  IMPORT &  EXPORT  TRADE

1850 1851 1852 1853 1854 1855 1856 1857 1858 1859 1860 1861 1862 1863 1864 1865 1866 1867 1868 1869 1870 1871 1872 1873 1874 1875 1876 1877 1878 1879

| | |
|---|---|
| 10.000.000 | 10 000 000 |
| 9.900.000 | 9 900 000 |
| 9.800.000 | 9 800 000 |
| 9.700.000 | 9 700 000 |
| 9.600.000 | 9 600 000 |
| 9.500.000 | 9 500 000 |
| 9.400.000 | 9 400 000 |
| 9.300.000 | 9 300 000 |
| 9.200.000 | 9 200 000 |
| 9.100.000 | 9 100 000 |
| 9.000.000 | 9 000 000 |
| 8.900.000 | 8 900 000 |
| 8.800.000 | 8 800 000 |
| 8.700.000 | 8 700 000 |
| 8.600.000 | 8 600 000 |
| 8.500.000 | 8 500 000 |
| 8.400.000 | 8 400 000 |
| 8.300.000 | 8 300 000 |
| 8.200.000 | 8 200 000 |
| 8.100.000 | 8 100 000 |
| 8.000.000 | 8 000 000 |
| 7.900.000 | 7 900 000 |
| 7.800.000 | 7 800 000 |
| 7.700.000 | 7 700 000 |
| 7.600.000 | 7 600 000 |
| 7.500.000 | 7 500 000 |
| 7.400.000 | 7 400 000 |
| 7.300.000 | 7 300 000 |
| 7.200.000 | 7 200 000 |
| 7.100.000 | 7 100 000 |
| 7.000.000 | 7 000 000 |
| 6.900.000 | 6 900 000 |
| 6.800.000 | 6 800 000 |
| 6.700.000 | 6 700 000 |
| 6.600.000 | 6 600 000 |
| 6.500.000 | 6 500 000 |
| 6.400.000 | 6 400 000 |
| 6.300.000 | 6 300 000 |
| 6.200.000 | 6 200 000 |
| 6.100.000 | 6 100 000 |
| 6.000.000 | 6 000 000 |
| 5.900.000 | 5 900 000 |
| 5.800.000 | 5 800 000 |
| 5.700.000 | 5 700 000 |
| 5.600.000 | 5 600 000 |
| 5.500.000 | 5 500 000 |
| 5.400.000 | 5 400 000 |
| 5.300.000 | 5 300 000 |
| 5.200.000 | 5 200 000 |
| 5.100.000 | 5 100 000 |
| 5.000.000 | 5 000 000 |
| 4.900.000 | 4 900 000 |
| 4.800.000 | 4 800 000 |
| 4.700.000 | 4 700 000 |
| 4.600.000 | 4 600 000 |
| 4.500.000 | 4 500 000 |
| 4.400.000 | 4 400 000 |
| 4.300.000 | 4 300 000 |
| 4.200.000 | 4 200 000 |
| 4.100.000 | 4 100 000 |
| 4.000.000 | 4 000 000 |
| 3.900.000 | 3 900 000 |
| 3.800.000 | 3 800 000 |
| 3.700.000 | 3 700 000 |
| 3.600.000 | 3 600 000 |
| 3.500.000 | 3 500 000 |
| 3.400.000 | 3 400 000 |
| 3.300.000 | 3 300 000 |
| 3.200.000 | 3 200 000 |
| 3.100.000 | 3 100 000 |
| 3.000.000 | 3 000 000 |
| 2.900.000 | 2 900 000 |
| 2.800.000 | 2 800 000 |
| 2.700.000 | 2 700 000 |
| 2.600.000 | 2 600 000 |
| 2.500.000 | 2 500 000 |
| 2.400.000 | 2 400 000 |
| 2.300.000 | 2 300 000 |
| 2.200.000 | 2 200 000 |
| 2.100.000 | 2 100 000 |
| 2.000.000 | 2 000 000 |
| 1.900.000 | 1 900 000 |
| 1.800.000 | 1 800 000 |
| 1.700.000 | 1 700 000 |
| 1.600.000 | 1 600 000 |
| 1.500.000 | 1 500 000 |
| 1.400.000 | 1 400 000 |
| 1.300.000 | 1 300 000 |
| 1.200.000 | 1 200 000 |
| 1.100.000 | 1 100 000 |
| 1.000.000 | 1 000 000 |
| 900.000 | 900 000 |
| 800.000 | 800 000 |
| 700.000 | 700 000 |
| 600.000 | 600 000 |
| 500.000 | 500 000 |
| 400.000 | 400 000 |
| 300.000 | 300 000 |
| 200.000 | 200 000 |
| 100.000 | 100 000 |
| 000.000 | 000 000 |

POPULATION ____ SHIPPING ____ EXPORTS ____ IMPORTS ____ COMBINED EXPORTS & IMPORTS ____ £

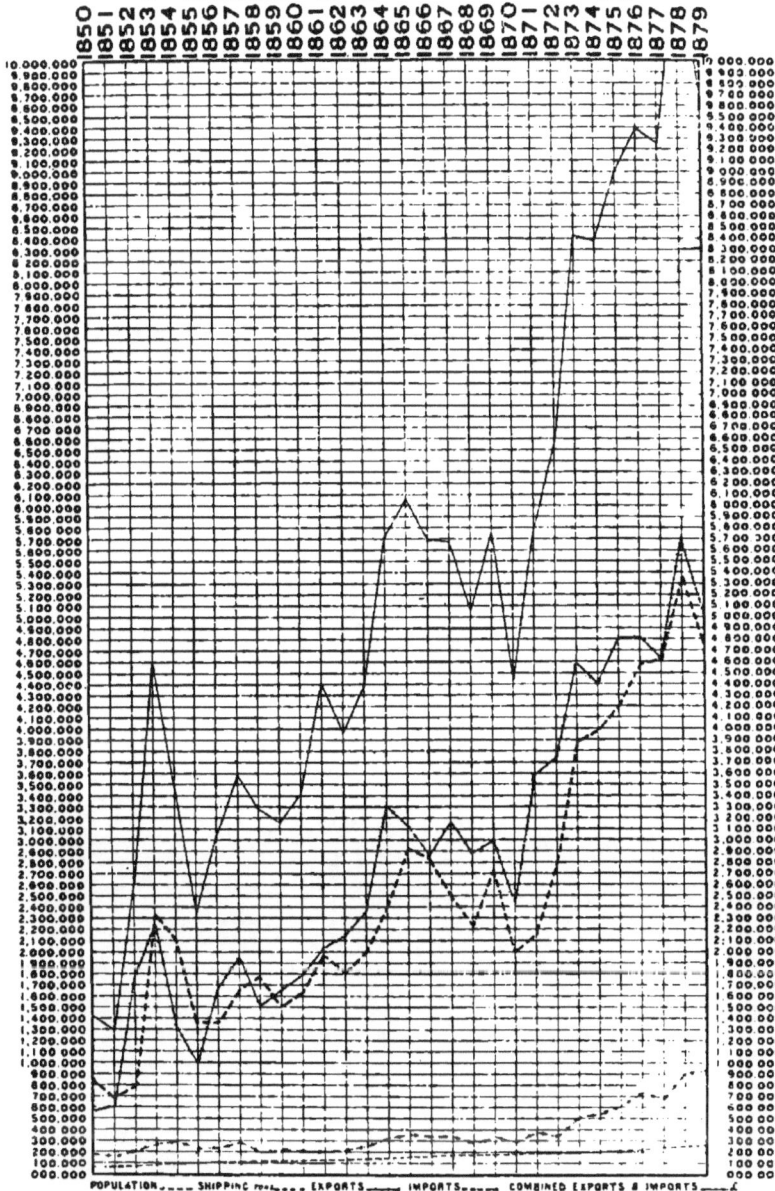

SURVEYOR GENERAL'S OFFICE, ADELAIDE. Frazer S Crawford, Photo-Lithographer

two millions (1,988,000); while, owing to a bad harvest, the least valuable is that of 1879, which, however, was considerably over one and a half million (1,648,000), comprising over 70,000 tons of flour and 442,000 quarters of wheat. The harvest of 1879-80 has been fairly good, and the area under wheat has so largely increased within the last few years (see page 36) that the export of breadstuffs during the present year will, in all probability, reach 300,000 tons, valued at nearly two and three-quarter millions sterling. The great bulk of the crop is shipped to the United Kingdom; but New South Wales, Queensland, Cape Town, Mauritius, New Caledonia, and several eastern ports also receive large consignments of flour. The price of wheat at Port Adelaide during the last five years has varied from 3s. 9d. to 8s. 2d. per bushel.

2. Wool was probably the first product exported, and is now second only to breadstuffs in importance. The increase has been especially marked during the last ten years, and in 1878 the value of the export amounted to over one and three-quarter millions sterling (£1,833,000) for fifty-six and a-half million lbs. In 1879 it stood at a little under one and three-quarter millions sterling (£1,694,000) for 43,149,981 lbs. The season 1879-80 has been a good one, and the value of the export for 1880 is expected to be considerably in advance of that of the previous year. Nearly all South Australian wool is shipped direct to London by steam or sailing vessels.

3. Copper and Copper Ore to the value of sixteen and a half millions sterling have been exported since 1843, but during the last three years the low price has considerably reduced the export, which in 1879 was only £351,388.

4. Miscellaneous Products.—In addition to the above chief staples, a variety of minor articles of produce are annually exported. The following were the principal items during 1879:—Tallow, 1,559 tons, £42,687 ; sheepskins, £30,000 ; bark, 3,740 tons, £26,000 ; wine, 47,000 gallons, £16,000 ; horses and sheep, each, £11,000; eggs, £9,000; jams, 327,000lbs., leather, £8,000 ; fresh fruit, £6,000 ; preserved meat, gum, and hay and chaff, each £5,000 ; hides, £4,000; biscuits and reaping-machines, each £2,000; soap and potatoes, each £1,800 ; almonds, £1,500 ; slate, salt, and other articles to a small value.

### 3.—Nature of Imports.

Full information of the nature of the import trade will be found in the "Statistical Register," lying on the table in the Court. The chief heads in order of value are—Between £200,000 and £300,000, raw sugar, apparel and slops, Government stores, greasy wool, drapery, cotton piece goods; between £200,000 and £100,000, washed wool, tea, bags, deals and battens, boots and shoes, coal; between £100,000 and £50,000, gold specie, galvanized iron, beer, tweeds, spirits, hardware, malt, books, fancy goods, furniture, drugs;

between £50,000 and £20,000, tools, woollen piece goods, potatoes, oats, candles, preserved fish, bar and rod iron, stationery, tobacco, boards, horses, machinery, printing paper, moleskins, wine, earthen and china ware, butter, cheese, musical instruments, ammunition, clocks and watches, copper, carpeting and druggeting, flannel piece goods; between £20,000 and £10,000, raw coffee, hops, leather, horned cattle, pearl shells, blankets, jewellery, kerosine, ploughshares, glassware, woodware, canvas, engines, cements, tanks, paints, sewing machines, brushware, carriages, rope and cordage, dried currants, pickles, and rum.

## 4.—*Direction of Trade.*

Of the total imports in 1879, over a half (£2,719,000) came from the United Kingdom; nearly three-quarters of a million worth from Victoria; £623,000 from New South Wales; nearly a quarter of a million from Mauritius; £129,000 from Western Australia; £245,000 from India and from the United States of America; between £90,000 and £50,000 worth came from China, New Zealand, Tasmania, and Norway and Sweden; about £30,000 from Queensland and Canada; £20,000 from Java; £8,000 from Bourbon; £2,000 from Germany; £1,000 from Egypt; and minor values from Port Darwin, the Cape, Hong Kong, and Natal.

Of the total exports in 1879, nearly two-thirds

(£2,845,000) went to the United Kingdom; £800 to Canada; £700,000 to New South Wales; £400,000 to Victoria ; under a quarter of a million to the Cape and to Queensland ; £116,000 to Western Australia ; £65,000 to Natal ; £50,000 to Mauritius ; £43,000 to New Caledonia ; £35,000 to New Zealand; £25,000 each to India and to Java ; £15,000 to Port Darwin ; £7,000 to Peru ; £4,500 to Hong Kong ; £2,500 to Tasmania and to St. Helena ; £1,700 to Ceylon ; and small values to the United States and to Singapore.

### 5.—*Shipping.*

Eleven hundred vessels, representing 468,000 tons, entered inwards at ports in the province in 1879, as against 1,040 vessels, with 465,000 tons, cleared out-wards. Direct steam communication between London and Adelaide is maintained by the Orient and P. & O. Companies, each of which dispatches one of their magnificent steamers—ranging from 2,500 to 5,000 tons—fortnightly; besides which, other steamers visit Adelaide occasionally. Steamers run twice a week between Adelaide and Melbourne, and there are now two more going to Sydney, one of which calls at Tasmania *en route.* Three lines of fine clipper ships, ranging from 800 to 1,800 tons register each, trade regularly between London and Adelaide, and there are also a large number of barques, schooners, and other craft in the intercolonial trade.

## 6.—*The River Murray Trade.*

South Australian enterprise opened the River Murray to navigation in 1853, and, subsequently, its great tributaries, the Darling and Murrumbidgee. Since the opening of these rivers, the whole of the immense tract of pastoral country known as the Riverina has been heavily stocked, producing now about 200,000 bales of wool annually. Of this river wool, over 30,000 tons were brought into South Australia in 1879, partly by the railroad from Morgan to Port Adelaide, partly by small steamers through the mouth of the Murray, partly by tramroad from Goolwa, at the Murray mouth, to Port Victor. The producing power of the Riverina country is capable of considerable expansion. The mouth of the Murray has been pronounced unimprovable, except at much cost; but, to facilitate the trade, large harbor works are being constructed at Port Victor, connected with the Murray mouth by a railroad some nine miles long.

## 7.—*The Tariff.*

Although the highest duties have for the most part been placed on articles which can be manufactured in the colony, the existing tariff was passed for the purpose of raising revenue, and not with a view to protection. Most articles of drapery, furniture, carriages, drugs, earthenware, jewellery, certain kinds of leather and leather goods, stationery and fancy goods, and fish and meat in pickle or brine, are charged

10 per cent. *ad valorem*, while engines not exceeding
60 horse power and agricultural implements pay 5
per cent. A number of articles are placed on the
free list.

For the benefit of merchants and other persons
wishing to trade with the colony the following complete list of dutiable goods is subjoined:—

### The Tariff of South Australia.

#### (Act No. 34 of 1876.—July 25, 1876.)

|  | s. | d. |
|---|---|---|
| Arrowroot, maizena, cornflour, sago, tapioca; pearl barley, split peas; biscuits; candles; dried, preserved, and salted fish and meats (except in brine or other pickle); preserved vegetables; blue; starch; glue—per lb. .. | 0 | 1 |
| Ale, porter, spruce, or other beer; cider, perry; vinegar, limejuice cordial (not being spirituous)—per gallon .. | 0 | 9 |
| Bags and sacks (being new), viz., bran, gunny, ore, un-enumerated—per dozen .. .. .. .. | 0 | 0 |
| Corn and flour (three bushels and over)—per dozen .. | 0 | 6 |
| Woolpacks—per dozen .. .. .. .. .. | 3 | 0 |
| Candied fruits, confectionery; dried fruits (except cocoa-nuts); bacon, cheese, hams; jams, jellies, preserves, cordials (not being spirituous), syrups; maccaroni, vermicelli, mustard, pepper, spices—per lb. or pint .. | 0 | 2 |
| Coffee (raw), cocoa, chocolate; hops; tea; sporting powder (except in casks)—per lb. .. .. .. .. | 0 | 3 |
| Cement, plaster of paris—per barrel .. .. .. | 2 | 0 |
| Chicory, coffee (roast or ground)—per lb .. .. .. | 0 | 4 |
| Doors and frames—each .. .. .. .. .. | 2 | 6 |
| Sashes—per pair .. .. .. .. .. .. | 2 | 6 |
| Fruits (bottled), pickles, sauces, salad oils—per dozen re-puted quarts .. .. .. .. .. .. | 2 | 0 |
| Fruits (bottled), pickles, sauces, salad oils—per dozen re-puted pints .. .. .. .. .. .. | 1 | 0 |
| Fruits (bottled), pickles, sauces, salad oils (smaller sizes)—per dozen.. .. .. .. .. .. | 0 | 9 |

|  | s. | d. |
|---|---|---|
| Iron, corrugated, galvanized (including galvanized iron wire)—per ton | 30 | 0 |
| Iron, galvanized, manufactures—per cwt. | 3 | 0 |
| Iron pipes, gates, fencing, and posts—per ton | 30 | 0 |
| Iron wire, iron girders—per ton | 20 | 0 |
| Kerosine—per gallon | 0 | 3 |
| Lead (pipe and sheet), shot—per cwt. | 2 | 6 |
| Malt—per bushel | 0 | 6 |
| Nails, screws, paints —per cwt. | 2 | 0 |
| Cordage, rope, spunyarn (except raw yarn, used for manufactures)—per cwt. | 3 | 0 |
| Oils (except cod and whale oils), turpentine, naphtha, varnish—per gallon | 0 | 6 |
| Opium—per lb. | 10 | 0 |
| Paper, wrapping (brown and whitey-brown), and paper bags—per cwt. | 3 | 4 |
| Playing cards—per dozen packs | 3 | 0 |
| Potatoes—per cwt. | 0 | 6 |
| Sarsaparilla (if not containing more than 25 per cent. of proof spirit)—per liquid gallon | 4 | 0 |
| Salt (except rock salt), saltpetre; soda (except caustic and silicate), soap—per ton | 20 | 0 |
| Spirits—Brandy, rum, gin, whisky, geneva, or strong waters of any kind or strength, including spirituous compounds, bitters, cordials, or strong waters sweetened or mixed with any article not exceeding the strength of proof by Sykes's hydrometer, and so on, in proportion, for any greater strength than the strength of proof—per gallon | 10 | 0 |
| Spirits—Wine, containing more than 35 per cent. of proof spirit in proportion to strength—per gallon | 10 | 0 |
| Spirits—Methylated—per gallon | 0 | 3 |
| Sugar, molasses, and treacle; rice—per cwt. | 3 | 0 |
| Tobacco, manufactured—per lb. | 2 | 0 |
| Tobacco, unmanufactured—per lb. | 0 | 9 |
| Tobacco, destroyed for sheepwash—per lb. | 0 | 3 |
| Tobacco, cigars, snuff—per lb. | 5 | 0 |
| Wine, sparkling—per gallon | 6 | 0 |
| Wine, other—per gallon | 4 | 0 |

|                                                                      | s. | d. |
|----------------------------------------------------------------------|----|----|
| Wood—Battens, deals, and planks, spar—per 40 cubic feet              | 2  | 6  |
| Wood—Architraves, skirtings, mouldings—per 100 lineal feet           | 1  | 6  |
| Wood—Boards, 3/8 to 1¹/₂in., rough or planed, tongued and grooved—per 100 superficial feet.. | 1 | 6 |
| Wood—Laths—per 1,000                                                 | 1  | 0  |
| Wood–Shingles—per 1,000..                                            | 0  | 6  |
| Wood—Palings—per 100                                                 | 0  | 6  |

On all imported goods included in the following list an *ad valorem* duty of 10 per cent., viz.:—

Drapery (except cotton and linen piece goods and woollen piece goods, not otherwise enumerated), haberdashery, hosiery, furs, gloves; millinery; hats, caps, bonnets; apparel and slops (except moleskin clothing); blankets, rugs, quilts, towels; boots, shoes, goloshes, portmanteaus, leather and carpet bags; umbrellas, parasols.

Furniture, carpeting, hearth rugs, mats, matting, oil and floor cloth; cornices, gilt mouldings, looking glasses; mantelpieces; paperhangings; iron bedsteads, safes, and doors; grates, stoves, ovens, fenders, fireirons; arms, ammunition; cutlery; tinware, japannedware; woodware (including bellows, picture frames, and washing-machines), turnery, and carved wood.

Carriages, carts, wagons, and vehicles of every description; wheels.

Drugs (except gum arabic), druggists' ware, chemicals (except bluestone and sulphuric acid), patent medicines; perfumery, brushes, combs, scented and fancy soaps, essences (not being spirituous compounds).

Earthenware, brownware, china; glass, glassware, glass bottles (except ordinary wine, beer, ginger beer, and sodawater bottles, and syphons), lamps; marble, stone, slate (wrought), tiles and bricks (except fire and bath bricks).

Jewellery, plate, plated goods; clocks, watches; musical instruments.

Leather (except patent and enamelled, and kid, hogskins, levant, morocco, roans, satins, and skivers), saddlery and harness (made up), whips, walking-sticks; tents, tarpaulins; boot uppers and leggings.

Stationery, manufactured (including account books, printed cheques and forms, bill-heads, and other printed or ruled paper); fancy goods, toys, brushware ; basket and wickerware ; tobacco pipes, tobacconists' ware.

Fish and meat, in pickle or brine.

On all imported goods included in the following list an *ad valorem* duty of 5 per cent., viz. :—

All cloths and tweeds in the piece.

Implements, viz. :—Engines not exceeding sixty horse-power, iron and brass castings, and wrought iron ; forged work used in the manufacture of steam engines ; pumps, iron and brass, exceeding 3in. bore ; boilers for steam engines and steam purposes ; chaffcutters ; corn-crushers, grain-sowers ; horse-powers ; mowing-machines ; reaping-machines, scarifiers, horse-rakes, ploughs, harrows, moulding-boards, ploughshares.

[N.B.—In all cases where duty is charged at per gallon, one dozen reputed quart bottles will be taken as two gallons, and one dozen reputed pint bottles as one gallon.]

## 8.—*Manufactures.*

Within the past few years local industries have largely increased in number and efficiency. Most of them have their raw material at hand in the produce of the country, and are engaged in supplying local demands rather than in exporting.

The chief manufactories are—Steam mills, 113 ; winemaking establishments, 100 ; agricultural implement works, 43 ; tanneries and fellmongeries, 40 ; boot and shoe factories, brickyards, and breweries, each 25 ; sawmills, aerated water and cordial factories, and coachbuilders' shops, each 20 ; limekilns, 6 ; clothing factories, 13 ; besides soap and candle factories, bone-dust mills, glue and size works, ship and boat building yards, potteries and tile and pipe works, gas works, dye works, rope-walks, brush manufactories, biscuit bakeries, jam and preserve and confectionery manufactories, dried fruit and olive oil factories, and ice works.

Among other miscellaneous local productions and manufactures are—Barilla, billiard tables, baking powder, blacking, cayenne pepper, cement, cigars, fibre, plaster of paris, washing-machines, sauces and pickles, salt, safety fuses, gas stoves, iron safes, bedsteads, galvanized iron, tinware, and nickel-plating.

———◆———

# AVERAGE RATES OF WAGES
## IN
# SOUTH AUSTRALIA
## FOR TEN YEARS

| OCCUPATION | | | 1870 | 1871 | 1872 | 1873 | 1874 | 1875 | 1876 | 1877 | 1878 | 1879 |
|---|---|---|---|---|---|---|---|---|---|---|---|---|
| **DOMESTIC** | | | | | | | | | | | | |
| GENERAL SERVANTS | with board and lodging | per annum | 40 | 40 | 40 | 43 | 45 | 50 | 43 | 45 | 43 | 43 |
| Do Do | female with bd | " " | 26 | 26 | 27 | 29 | 29 | 29 | 29 | 29 | 28 | 28 |
| COOKS | male | per week | 25.0 | 30.0 | 35.0 | 30.0 | 38.0 | 36.0 | 30.0 | 30.0 | 27.0 | 27.0 |
| Do | female | " " | 14.0 | 15.0 | 15.0 | 15.0 | 16.0 | 17.0 | 16.0 | 16.0 | 16.0 | 16.0 |
| HOUSE & KITCHEN MAIDS | " " | " " | 9.0 | 9.0 | 10.0 | 10.0 | 10.5 | 10.6 | 10.0 | 10.0 | 10.0 | 10.0 |
| LAUNDRESSES | " " | " " | 12.0 | 12.0 | 12.0 | 12.0 | 13.0 | 14.0 | 14.0 | 14.0 | 14.0 | 14.0 |
| **FARM & DAIRY** | | | | | | | | | | | | |
| MAN & WIFE | with board and lodging | per annum | 46 | 45 | 50 | 55 | 58 | 60 | 58 | 58 | 58 | 58 |
| SINGLE MEN | " " | " " | 40 | 40 | 42 | 45 | 50 | 52 | 49 | 50 | 48 | 48 |
| HARVEST HANDS | " " | per week | 1.10 | 1.10 | 1.10 | 1.10 | 1.10 | 1.15 | 1.5 | 1.6 | 1.8 | 1.8 |
| MILKMEN | " " | " " | 15.0 | 15.0 | 15.0 | 17.0 | 20.0 | 20.0 | 18.0 | 18.0 | 18.6 | 18.6 |
| DAIRYMAIDS | " " | " " | 10.0 | 10.0 | 10.0 | 10.0 | 10.0 | 11.0 | 12.0 | 11.0 | 11.0 | 11.0 |
| DAIRY WORK | " " | " " | 23.0 | 23.0 | 23.0 | 23.0 | 30.0 | 30.0 | 27.0 | 27.0 | 27.0 | 27.0 |
| GOOD CHEESEMAKERS | " " | " " | 10.0 | 10.0 | 10.0 | 10.0 | 12.0 | 12.0 | 12.0 | 12.0 | 12.0 | 12.0 |
| **HOTEL** | | | | | | | | | | | | |
| BARMEN | with board and lodging | per week | 22.0 | 21.0 | 21.0 | 25.0 | 30.0 | 30.0 | 28.0 | 28.0 | 28.0 | 28.0 |
| BARMAIDS | " " | " " | 14.0 | 15.0 | 15.0 | 15.0 | 17.0 | 17.0 | 17.0 | 17.0 | 17.0 | 17.0 |
| BOOTS & MEN SERVANTS | " " | " " | 14.0 | 15.0 | 16.0 | 17.0 | 18.0 | 20.0 | 18.0 | 18.0 | 18.0 | 18.0 |
| OSTLERS | " " | " " | 15.0 | 15.0 | 16.0 | 17.0 | 18.0 | 20.0 | 18.0 | 18.0 | 18.0 | 18.0 |
| STABLE HELPS YOUTHS | " " | " " | 12.0 | 12.0 | 12.0 | 14.0 | 14.0 | 14.0 | 12.0 | 12.0 | 12.0 | 12.0 |
| **SHEEP & CATTLE STATIONS** | | | | | | | | | | | | |
| SHEPHERDS | rations with double rations | per annum | 30 | 35 | 37 | 40 | 40 | 40 | 40 | 40 | 40 | 40 |
| Do | single & hutkeeper one ration each | " " | 30 | 35 | 37 | 40 | 40 | 40 | 40 | 40 | 40 | 40 |
| Do | single keeping his own hut & rations | " " | 39 | 35 | 39 | 45 | 45 | 50 | 50 | 50 | 50 | 50 |
| HUTKEEPERS | with rations | " " | 26 | 28 | 26 | 31 | 32 | 32 | 30 | 30 | 36 | 36 |
| LAMBMINDERS | requires about 3 months + do | " " | 26 | 26 | 31 | 39 | 39 | 39 | 39 | 39 | 39 | 39 |
| MAN & WIFE | " " | " " | 50 | 50 | 52 | 55 | 65 | 60 | 60 | 60 | 60 | 60 |
| MEN FOR GENERAL WORK | with rations | " " | 40 | 40 | 45 | 47 | 50 | 52 | 50 | 50 | 50 | 50 |
| BUSH CARPENTERS | " " | " " | 80 | 60 | 65 | 70 | 78 | 90 | 85 | 90 | 90 | 90 |
| MEN COOKS | " " | " " | 45 | 40 | 45 | 52 | 52 | 52 | 52 | 52 | 52 | 52 |
| TEAMSTERS | " " | " " | 45 | 45 | 45 | 52 | 52 | 52 | 52 | 52 | 52 | 52 |
| SHEEPOROVERS | " " | " " | 52 | 52 | 52 | 60 | 80 | 76 | 85 | 65 | 65 | 65 |
| STOCKMEN | " " | " " | 60 | 55 | 55 | 60 | 60 | 85 | 60 | 60 | 60 | 60 |
| COLTBREAKERS | " " | " " | 60 | 55 | 55 | 60 | 65 | 70 | 70 | 70 | 70 | 70 |
| WATER DRAWERS | " " | " " | 39 | 39 | 39 | 45 | 45 | 50 | 45 | 45 | 45 | 45 |
| WELL SINKERS | average earnings | per week | 35.0 | 30.0 | 30.0 | 35.0 | 37.0 | 42.0 | 42.0 | 42.0 | 42.8 | 42.6 |
| HUT BUILDERS | " " | " " | 35.0 | 30.0 | 30.0 | 35.0 | 39.0 | 40.0 | 40.0 | 40.0 | 40.0 | 40.0 |
| WOOL PRESSERS | " " | " " | 35.0 | 30.0 | 30.0 | 30.0 | 30.0 | 30.0 | 35.0 | 35.0 | 35.0 | 35.0 |
| SHEEP SHEARERS | " " | per 100 | 15.0 | 18.0 | 18.0 | 18.0 | 18.0 | 20.0 | 18.6 | 18.6 | 18.6 | 18.5 |
| **TRADES &c** | | | | | | | | | | | | |
| BAKERS | with board and lodging | per week | 4.6 | 4.6 | 4.6 | 5.0 | 5.8 | 5.6 | 5 | 5.6 | 5.6 | 5.6 |
| BLACKSMITHS | without do | " " | 7.6 | 7.6 | 8.0 | 8.6 | 9.0 | 9.0 | 9.0 | 9.0 | 9.0 | 9.0 |
| BRICKLAYERS | " " | " " | 8.0 | 8.0 | 9.0 | 9.0 | 9.0 | 8.0 | 9.0 | 9.0 | 9.0 | 9.0 |
| BRICKMAKERS | " " | per 1000 | 12.0 | 12.0 | 12.0 | 12.0 | 12.0 | 12.0 | 12.0 | 12.0 | 12.0 | 12.0 |
| BUTCHERS | with board and lodging | per week | 4.6 | 4.6 | 4.6 | 5.0 | 5.0 | 5.0 | 5.0 | 5.0 | 5.0 | 5.0 |
| CABINET MAKERS | without do | " " | 8.0 | 8.0 | 8.0 | 8.0 | 9.0 | 9.6 | 9.6 | 9.6 | 9.6 | 9.6 |
| CARPENTERS | " " | " " | 8.0 | 8.0 | 8.0 | 8.0 | 9.0 | 9.0 | 9.0 | 9.0 | 9.0 | 9.0 |
| CARRIAGE BUILDERS | " " | " " | 9.0 | 9.0 | 9.0 | 9.0 | 9.0 | 9.0 | 9.0 | 9.0 | 9.0 | 9.0 |
| CIGAR MAKERS | " " | " " | | | 7.0 | 7.0 | 7.0 | 8.0 | 8.6 | 8.6 | 8.6 | 8.6 |
| COOPERS | " " | " " | 8.0 | 8.0 | 8.0 | 8.0 | 7.6 | 7.6 | 7.6 | 7.6 | 9.6 | 9.6 |
| COLLAR MAKERS | " " | " " | 10.0 | 10.0 | 10.0 | 10.0 | 10.6 | 10.0 | 10.0 | 10.0 | 10.0 | 10.0 |
| DAY LABORERS | " " | " " | 5.6 | 6.0 | 6.0 | 7.0 | 7.6 | 7.6 | 6.6 | 6.6 | 6.6 | 6.6 |
| FRENCH POLISHERS | " " | " " | 8.0 | 8.0 | 8.0 | 8.0 | 8.0 | 8.0 | 7.6 | 7.6 | 7.6 | 7.6 |
| GALVANIZED IRON WORKERS | " " | " " | 8.0 | 8.0 | 8.0 | 8.6 | 9.0 | 9.0 | 8.0 | 8.0 | 8.0 | 8.0 |
| HARNESS MAKERS | " " | " " | 8.0 | 9.0 | 8.6 | 8.6 | 9.0 | 8.0 | 7.0 | 7.0 | 7.0 | 7.0 |
| JEWELLERS | " " | " " | 9.0 | 9.0 | 9.6 | 9.6 | 9.6 | 10.0 | 10.0 | 10.0 | 10.0 | 10.0 |
| MACHINISTS | " " | " " | 9.0 | 9.0 | 9.6 | 9.6 | 9.6 | 10.0 | 10.0 | 10.0 | 10.0 | 10.0 |
| MASONS | " " | " " | 8.0 | 8.6 | 9.0 | 9.0 | 9.0 | 9.0 | 9.0 | 9.6 | 9.6 | 9.6 |
| MILLERS | " " | " " | 9.0 | 9.0 | 9.0 | 9.0 | 9.0 | 9.0 | 9.6 | 9.6 | 9.6 | 9.6 |
| MINERS | " " | " " | 6.0 | 6.3 | 6.3 | 6.3 | 6.3 | 6.3 | 6.0 | 5.6 | 5.6 | 5.6 |
| PAINTERS & GLAZIERS | " " | " " | 8.6 | 9.0 | 9.0 | 9.0 | 9.0 | 9.0 | 9.0 | 9.0 | 9.0 | 9.0 |
| PLASTERERS | " " | " " | 8.0 | 8.0 | 9.6 | 9.0 | 10.0 | 10.0 | 10.0 | 10.0 | 10.0 | 10.0 |
| SADDLERS | " " | " " | 9.0 | 9.0 | 9.0 | 9.0 | 9.6 | 8.6 | 10.0 | 10.0 | 10.0 | 10.0 |
| SAWYERS | " " | per 100 ft | 9.0 | 9.0 | 9.6 | 9.6 | 9.6 | 10.0 | 10.0 | 10.0 | 10.0 | 10.0 |
| SHOEMAKERS | " " | per pair | 6.0 | 6.6 | 6.6 | 6.9 | 7.0 | 7.0 | 7.6 | 7.6 | 7.6 | 7.6 |
| TAILORS | " " | per hour | 9 | | 10 | 10 | 10 | 11 | 1.0 | 1.0 | 1.0 | 1.0 |
| TANNERS | " " | per week | 8.6 | 8.6 | 8.6 | 8.6 | 8.6 | 8.6 | 8.6 | 8.6 | 8.6 | 8.6 |
| TINSMITHS | " " | " " | 8.0 | 8.0 | 8.0 | 7.6 | 7.6 | 6.6 | 6.6 | 6.6 | 6.6 | 6.6 |
| UPHOLSTERERS | " " | " " | 10.0 | 10.0 | 10.0 | 10.0 | 10.0 | 10.0 | 10.0 | 10.0 | 10.0 | 10.0 |
| WHEELWRIGHTS | " " | " " | 8.6 | 9.0 | 9.0 | 9.0 | 9.0 | 9.0 | 9.0 | 9.0 | 9.0 | 9.0 |

Scale of rations per week — 10lb flour, 13lb meat, 2lb sugar, 2lb tea.

Married farm labourers have cottage provided rent free, and fuel and water gratis.

Servants are conveyed up country at employers' cost.

# CHAP. VI.—FINANCE.

## 1.—*The National Debt.*

From time to time moneys have been raised by loan for the carrying out of reproductive public works (page 44). Many of these will, no doubt, ultimately not only pay for maintenance, working expenses, and interest on outlay, but will also yield a profit. At first it is impossible they can do so. In the meantime, however, they are of direct advantage to the country in increasing the value of property, and extending the margin of cultivation and of settlement.

The amount of the Public Debt outstanding at end of 1879 was over $9\frac{3}{4}$ millions sterling ($£9,882,900$); see " Statistical Register." The earlier debentures issued, to the amount of nearly a million and a half, bore interest at 6 per cent. Susequently $£400,000$ worth were issued at 5 per cent.; but of late years only 4 per cent. has been paid. Over eight millions have been raised at this rate. The mean price of South Australian 4 per cents. during the first six months of the present year has been 97. The currency of the bond is generally thirty years. Redemptions to the amount of $£850,000$ have been made since the first issue of bonds in 1854. The total rate of indebtedness per head of the population is about $£21$.

E

Against this indebtedness of nearly ten millions may
be set nearly five millions due to the Government
by credit selectors, and public works to the value of
nearly eight millions.

## 2.—Revenue and Expenditure.

Exclusive of the Public Loan Account, which is
kept separately, the General Revenue for the financial
year ending June 30, 1880 amounted to over a million
and a three-quarters sterling (£1,831,164), as against
an almost equal expenditure, £1,853,113.

The chief heads of receipt were—Sale of Crown
Lands and Interest on Credit Sales, £531,610;
Customs and Excise, £510,796; Probate and Succession Duties, £12,200; Railways and Tramways,
£364,855; Post and Telegraphs, £130,929; Water-
works, £48,727; Marine, £12,592; Rents of Crown
Lands, £74,243; together with education fees, business licences, and reimbursements-in-aid.

The chief heads of expenditure were — Public
Works £293,457; Immigration, £24,951; Interest
and Redemption of Bonds, £397,364; Survey of
Crown Lands, £70,421.—The above items are paid
for out of the sums derived from the sale of Crown
Lands; Railways and Tramways, £260,530; Post
and Telegraphs, £167,369; Education, £103,114.
The balance is made up by the ordinary expenses
necessary to the maintenance of Government in all
civilised communities.

The total taxation in 1879 was about £2 per head of the population. Nearly the whole of it is raised by Customs Duties, which amounted to £1 19s.; the balance being made up by Probate and Succession Duties.

### 3.—Banking.

Eight banking institutions carry on business within the province, viz.:—The Bank of South Australia, National Bank of Australasia, Union Bank of Australia, Bank of Australasia; English, Scottish, and Australian Chartered Bank; Bank of Adelaide, Bank of New South Wales, and the Commercial Bank of South Australia. All of these have their head quarters at Adelaide, and there are over 100 branches and agencies in the principal sea-port and inland townships.

At the end of June, 1880, (quarterly return) the total average liabilities of the eight banks amounted to £4,555,045; assets, £7,370,531; amount of notes in circulation, not bearing interest, £474,570; bills in circulation, £12,944; balances due to other banks, £56,012; deposits, £4,011,518; capital stock, paid-up.

The assets consisted of coined gold, silver, and other metals, £922,849; gold and silver in bullion or ingots, £8,551; Government securities, £25,000; landed property and bank premises, £261,694; notes and bills of other banks, £50,199; balances due from other banks, £184,529; notes and bills discounted and other debts due to banks not enumerated, £5,917,706.

The rate of interest allowed to depositors varied from £5 per cent., at thirty days' notice, to £6 10s., and more usually £6, for twelve months.

The course of exchange was 1 per cent. premium for drafts on London at twenty days' sight, and $1/4$ to 1 per cent. premium for drafts at sight on neighboring colonies; on private bills purchased on London at sixty days $1/2$ per cent. discount, and on neighbouring colonies at sight $3/8$ and 1 per cent.

The rate of discount on local bills is—under 65 days, 8 per cent.; 65 to 95 days, 8 per cent.; 95 to 125 days, 9 per cent.; and over 125 days, 10 per cent.

# Chap. VII.—The Northern Territory.

## 1. Settlement.

The successful crossing of the centre of Australia from south to north by John McDouall Stuart, in 1862, led in due course to the annexation to South Australia of the extensive region between the 26th parallel of the southern latitude and the Indian Ocean, containing an area of 531,000 square miles.

The first settlement was at Adam Bay, at the mouth of the Adelaide River. These early attempts at colonising were unsuccessful, and later on Port Darwin was chosen as the nucleus of settlement.

## 2. Climate.

The climate of the Northern Territory is tropical, and there are but two seasons. The wet season begins towards the end of October, and lasts about five months. During January and February the rainfall is very heavy, and it is during this period that the heat is also most intense. The maximum temperature recorded at this time of year is 96°, and the minimum during the night 65°. During the remainder of the year the temperature is equable and cool, except just prior to the setting in of the rainy season. The sun is rarely shadowed by a cloud, and day after day there is a clear bright sky. During June and July the maximum temperature registered was 84°, and the minimum 56°. The annual rainfall registered at Port Darwin during the last nine years varies from 51in. to 80in., while the wet season rainfall for the same period ranges from 47in. to 77in. The sickness most prevalent amongst the settlers is a kind of intermittent fever, accompanied by ague. This complaint is very trying, though not really dangerous.

### 3. Physical Features.

North Australia is remarkable for the number and size of its rivers. The chief of these are the Adelaide, which empties itself into Adam Bay, and is navigable for a distance of 50 miles; the Roper, flowing westerly into the Gulf of Carpentaria, and is navigable for nearly 100 miles; the Victoria, in the western portion of the Territory, which can be navigated by small crafts at least 100 miles, and 40 by large ones; the Liverpool, the South and East Alligators, the Daly, which empties itself into Adam Bay, and many others.

### 4. Agriculture.

The character of the soil in so large an area is necessarily variable, but its general fertility is unquestionable. No difficulty is experienced in finding large blocks of rich land capable of growing tropical products in luxuriance. Maize grows pro-

fusely, and the experiments made justify the belief
that such articles as sugar, cotton, and indigo
would also prosper in many situations. Nearly all
kinds of tropical fruits and vegetables thrive and
flourish in these latitudes. The plaintain and banana
grow wherever they are stuck in the ground, and
produce excellent fruit. Cocoa-nut trees and pine-
apples, together with lemon and orange trees, flourish
in the Palmerston Botanic Garden. The " custard-
apple," the " papaya," the tamarind tree, the guava,
and the rosella, all thrive well. Splendid specimens
of the mango are obtained at Port Essington. In
vegetables the melon tribe succeeds admirably, and
grows as weeds in some places. The yam and sweet
potato have been cultivated with great success.
Arrowroot has been tried on a small scale and thrives
exceedingly well. It is believed that the tea plant
would grow well in certain districts, and the same
may be said of spices, but none have yet been planted.
Excellent sugar-cane is grown at the Government
Garden, and cotton raised there obtained the first
prize at the Sydney Exhibition. The cultivation of
Indian corn promises well, and couch grass and
buffalo grass both grow rapidly.

### 5. Pasture.

As to the pastoral capabilities of the Territory
there can be no doubt. Within the last three years
nearly 200,000 square miles of country have been

taken up by squatters. The existing regulations provide that the person who shall describe any country not previously applied for without the settled districts for pastoral purposes shall be entitled to a preferential right to a lease, for any period not exceeding 25 years, of any portion in one block of not less than 25 square miles nor more than 400 in extent, at an annual rental of 6d. per square mile for the first seven years, and 10s. per square mile for the remainder of the term, on condition that the run is declared stocked within a period of three years, at the rate of two head of great cattle, or ten head of small cattle for every square mile of country.

### 6. Gold Mining.

Gold mining has hitherto been the only industry carried on to any extent. Some splendid nuggets have occasionally been obtained from the alluvial diggings, and the quartz-crushing returns have in many cases shown from four to six ounces to the ton. The principal reefs at present open are the Stapleton Creek, Howley, John Bull, Yam Creek, Union, Extended Union, and Pine Creek.

The distance of these reefs from Port Darwin is over 100 miles, and the want of a good road has hitherto greatly impeded the development of the mines. That desideratum has at length been supplied, and now, by a steamer to Southport (25 miles), and thence to Yam Creek (90 miles) by an excellent road, com-

munication is open; and a weekly coach, carrying
nine persons, runs from Southport to Yam Creek.

A new alluvial diggings has just been started
(July, 1880) on the Margaret River, seven miles from
Yam Creek, where the Government Resident (Mr. E.
W. Price) reports "large quantities of gold are being
found" (13th July, 1880), indicating, he thinks,
"rich reefs in the neighboring hills." At these
diggings, on the 30th July, 1,100, Chinese and 50
Europeans were camped. "Some works were stopped
for want of water, but when the wet season comes a
large population is looked for." Trooper Wrinkler
reports a nugget of 42lbs. weight.

On the 2nd of August, twenty-six teams were
carting on the Southport and Yam Creek Road at
£16 per ton—horses and wagons being scarce, but
provisions abundant.

### 7. Population.

The population of the settlement is estimated at
about 400 whites, 30 Malays, and 2,040 Chinese.

### 8. Administration of Justice.

The Government Resident presides at a Circuit
Court, and has power to try all felonies (except
murder) and misdemeanors. A Local Court of Full
and Limited Jurisdiction is also held at Palmerston.

Return showing the Retail Prices of General Produce at the Markets in Adelaide in each alternate month of the Year 1879.

| Article | February | April | June | August | October | December |
|---|---|---|---|---|---|---|
| | s. d. | s. d. | s. d. | s. d. | s. d. | s. d. |
| **Bread and Flour—** | | | | | | |
| Bread, yeast ... 2lb. loaf | 0 3 to 0 3¼ | 0 3 to 0 3½ | 0 3 to 0 3½ | 0 3 to 0 3½ | 0 3¼ to 0 4 | 0 3¼ to 0 4 |
| Ditto, aerated ..2lb. loaf | — | 0 4 | 0 4 | 0 4 | 0 4 | 0 4 |
| Flour ...........per lb. | 0 2 | 0 2 | 0 2 | 0 2 | 0 2¼ | 0 2½ |
| **Meat—** | | | | | | |
| Beef .............lb. | 0 3 to 0 7 | 0 3 to 0 7 | 0 3 to 0 6 | 0 3 to 0 7 | 0 3 to 0 8 | 0 3 to 0 8 |
| Mutton ..........lb. | 0 1½ to 0 4 | 0 1½ to 0 4 | 0 1½ to 0 4 | 0 2 to 0 5 | 0 2 to 0 5 | 0 2 to 0 5 |
| Pork ............lb. | 0 7 to 0 8 | 0 7 to 0 8 | 0 7 to 0 8 | 0 7 to 0 8 | 0 8 to 0 9 | 0 8 to 0 9 |
| Veal.............lb. | 0 4 to 0 7 | 0 4 to 0 7 | 0 4 to 0 7 | 0 4 to 0 7 | 0 4 to 0 8 | 0 4 to 0 8 |
| **Dairy Produce—** | | | | | | |
| Bacon, colonial .....lb. | 0 11 | 1 0 | 0 10 | 0 10 | 0 9 | 0 10 |
| Butter, fresh .. ....lb. | 1 3 | 1 2 | 1 0 | 0 8 | 1 0 | 0 11 |
| Cheese ...........lb. | 0 8 | 0 8 | 0 7 | 0 8 | 0 9 | 0 7 |
| Ducks ...........pair | 5 6 | 6 0 | 5 0 | 6 0 | 6 0 | 5 0 |
| Eggs ...........dozen | 1 6 | 1 0 | 0 8 | 1 0 | 1 0 | 1 0 |
| Fowls ...........pair | 4 6 | 4 0 | 3 6 | 4 0 | 5 0 | 5 0 |
| Geese ...........each | 5 0 | 5 0 | 5 0 | 5 0 | 5 0 | 5 0 |

| Item | Unit |
|---|---|
| Ham | lb. |
| Honey | lb. |
| Lard | lb. |
| Milk | quart |
| Pigeons | pair |
| Rabbits | pair |
| Turkeys | each |
| **Fruit—** | |
| Pomegranates | dozen |
| Almonds | lb. |
| Quinces | bushel |
| Apples | bushel |
| Apricots | cwt. |
| Gooseberries | bushel |
| Citrons | bushel |
| Lemons | dozen |
| Cherries | dozen lbs. |
| Loquats | dozen lbs. |
| Damsons | bushel |
| Oranges | dozen |
| Figs | dozen |
| Pears | bushel |
| Grapes | dozen lbs. |
| Mulberries | lb. |
| Nectarines | dozen |
| Strawberries | lb. |
| Peaches | dozen |
| Walnuts | dozen lbs. |
| Plums | bushel |
| Raspberries | dozen lbs. |

*Retail Prices of General Produce at the Markets in Adelaide—continued.*

| Article | February | | April | | June | | August | | October | | December | |
|---|---|---|---|---|---|---|---|---|---|---|---|---|
| | s. d. | s. d. | s. d. | s. d. | s. d. | s. d. | s. d. | s. d. | s. d. | s. d. | s. d. | s. d. |
| Vegetables— | | | | | | | | | | | | |
| Artichokes .......... lb. | 0 1½ | | 0 1½ | 0 2 | | | | | | | 0 1½ | 0 2 |
| Beetroot ....... dozen | 2 0 | | 0 3 | | 2 0 | 3 0 | 2 0 | 3 0 | 1 0 | | 1 1 | 2 6 |
| Broad Beans .... bushel | 3 0 | | 3 2 | | 1 2 | | 1 2 | | 1 1 | | 2 2 | — |
| Carrots .. dozen bunches | 2 0 | 0 6 | 1 3 | 2 6 | 2 6 | 2 5 | 2 6 | 2 0 | 1 6 | | 1 6 | 0 0 |
| Cabbages ........ dozen | 2 0 | | 3 0 | 6 8 | 2 6 | 5 5 | 2 6 | 5 0 | 1 6 | 4 4 | 1 6 | 2 0 |
| Cauliflowers .... dozen | 2 0 | 6 0 | 4 3 | 8 4 | 2 6 | 4 5 | 2 6 | 5 5 | 1 6 | 5 4 | 1 6 | 2 0 |
| Celery ..... dozen sticks | 3 0 | | 3 3 | 4 4 | 2 0 | 4 5 | 2 0 | 5 5 | 2 0 | 4 0 | 1 1 | — |
| Chillies ............ lb. | 1 0 | | 1 1 | | 1 0 | | 1 0 | | 1 0 | | 1 1 | 6 0 |
| Cucumbers ...... dozen | 1 6 | | 0 6 | 3 0 | 0 8 | | 0 8 | 0 6 | 0 8 | | 5 0 | — |
| Horseradish ........ lb. | 0 6 | 5 0 | 0 4 | 0 0 | 0 4 | | 0 4 | 0 1 | 0 4 | 0 1 | 0 0 | 1 0 |
| Shalots .......... lb. | 0 4 | 8 0 | 0 9 | | 0 9 | 1 3 | 0 6 | 6 0 | 0 6 | | 0 0 | 12 0 |
| Lettuces ......... dozen | 0 9 | 1 0 | 0 6 | 1 0 | 0 0 | 14 0 | 0 0 | | 0 0 | 0 14 | 0 0 | — |
| Onions ........ cwt. | 8 6 | 10 8 | 10 0 | 12 0 | 12 0 | | 12 0 | | 12 0 | | 10 0 | — |
| Mint .... dozen bunches | 1 0 | 0 0 | 0 1 | | 0 1 | | 0 1 | | 0 1 | | 0 1 | — |
| Parsley .. dozen bunches | 2 0 | 2 6 | 2 0 | | 2 0 | 2 6 | 2 0 | | 2 0 | | 1 1 | — |
| Parsnips .. dozen bunches | 8 0 | | 5 0 | 6 0 | 0 0 | | 0 0 | | 4 0 | | 2 2 | — |
| Peas ............ bushel | 6 0 | 7 0 | 6 0 | 10 0 | 6 0 | | 0 0 | | 9 0 | | 9 0 | 3 0 |
| Potatoes ........ cwt. | | | 8 0 | 6 0 | 7 6 | | 8 0 | 13 0 | 12 0 | | 10 0 | 10 0 |
| Ditto, new ....... cwt. | 3 6 | 6 0 | 5 0 | 6 8 | 0 0 | 0 8 | 0 0 | 14 0 | 0 0 | | 6 0 | 9 8 |
| Trombones .... dozen | 0 6 | 6 0 | 1 0 | 0 1 | | 0 1 | 0 6 | 0 8 | 6 0 | 0 8 | 6 0 | 9 0 |
| Radishes . dozen bunches | 0 6 | 0 1 | 0 6 | 0 0 | 0 2 | | 0 2 | | 0 2 | | 0 0 | — |
| Tomatoes .... dozen lbs. | | | 0 2 | | 0 2 | 6 0 | 0 2 | 0 2 | 0 2 | 0 2 | 0 2 | 1 9 |
| Watercress . dozen bunches | 2 6 | 3 0 | 2 2 | 3 3 | 2 2 | | 6 0 | | 6 0 | | 6 0 | 1 3 |
| Turnips .. dozen bunches | 2 6 | 3 0 | 6 6 | 3 3 | 6 6 | | 6 6 | 0 2 | 6 6 | 0 1 | 3 0 | 2 3 |
| Rhubarb .... dozen lbs. | 2 0 | 0 0 | 0 2 | | 0 0 | | 0 1 | | 0 2 | | 2 0 | — |

*Decennial Return showing the Average Rates of Wages in the Province.*

| Occupation. | | 1870. | 1871. | 1872. | 1873. | 1874. | 1875. | 1876. | 1877. | 1878. | 1879. |
|---|---|---|---|---|---|---|---|---|---|---|---|
| **Domestic—** | | £ | £ | £ | £ | £ | £ | £ | £ | £ | £ |
| General servants, male, board and lodging..per annum | | 40 | 40 | 40 | 43 | 45 | 50 | 43 | 43 | 43 | 43 |
| " female " | | 26 | 26 | 27 | 29 | 29 | 29 | 28 | 28 | 28 | 28 |
| | | s. d. | s. d. | s. d. | s. d. | s. d. | s. d. | s. d. | s. d. | s. d. | s. d. |
| Cooks, male " per week | | 30 0 | 30 0 | 35 0 | 30 0 | 36 0 | 36 0 | 30 0 | 27 0 | 27 0 | 27 0 |
| " female " | | 14 0 | 15 0 | 15 0 | 15 0 | 16 0 | 17 0 | 16 0 | 16 0 | 16 0 | 16 0 |
| House and kitchen maids " | | 9 0 | 9 0 | 10 0 | 10 0 | 10 6 | 10 6 | 10 0 | 10 0 | 10 0 | 10 0 |
| Laundresses " | | 12 0 | 12 0 | 12 0 | 12 0 | 13 0 | 14 0 | 14 0 | 14 0 | 14 0 | 14 0 |
| **Farm and Dairy—** | | £ | £ | £ | £ | £ | £ | £ | £ | £ | £ |
| Man and wife, with board and lodging ....per annum | | 45 | 45 | 50 | 55 | 58 | 60 | 58 | 58 | 58 | 58 |
| Single men " .... | | 40 | 40 | 42 | 45 | 50 | 52 | 49 | 48 | 48 | 48 |
| Harvest hands ..... .. ............ per week | | — | — | — | — | — | 1 15 | 1 5 | 1 7¾ | 1 7¾ | 1 8 |
| | | s. d. | s. d. | s. d. | s. d. | s. d. | s. d. | s. d. | s. d. | s. d. | s. d. |
| Milkmen, with board and lodging | | 15 0 | 15 0 | 16 0 | 17 0 | 20 0 | 20 0 | 18 0 | 18 0 | 18 6 | 18 6 |
| Dairymaids " | | 10 0 | 10 0 | 10 0 | 10 0 | 11 0 | 12 0 | 11 0 | 11 0 | 11 0 | 11 0 |
| Dairywork, man and wife " | | 23 0 | 23 0 | 23 0 | 25 0 | 30 0 | 30 0 | 27 0 | 27 0 | 27 0 | 27 0 |
| Good cheesemakers " | | 10 0 | 11 0 | 10 0 | 10 0 | 12 0 | 12 0 | 12 0 | 12 0 | 12 0 | 12 0 |
| **Hotel—** | | s. d. | s. d. | s. d. | s. d. | s. d. | s. d. | s. d. | s. d. | s. d. | s. d. |
| Barmen, with board and lodging | | 22 0 | 21 0 | 21 0 | 25 0 | 30 0 | 30 0 | 28 0 | 28 0 | 28 0 | 28 0 |
| Barmaids " | | 14 0 | 15 0 | 15 0 | 15 0 | 17 0 | 17 0 | 17 0 | 17 0 | 17 0 | 17 0 |
| Boots and men servants " | | 14 0 | 15 0 | 16 0 | 17 0 | 18 0 | 20 0 | 18 0 | 18 0 | 18 0 | 18 0 |
| Ostlers " | | 15 0 | 15 0 | 16 0 | 17 0 | 18 0 | 20 0 | 18 0 | 18 0 | 18 0 | 18 0 |
| Stable helps, youths " | | — | — | — | — | — | 14 0 | 12 0 | 12 0 | 12 0 | 12 0 |

*Average Rates of Wages in the Province—continued.*

| Occupation. | 1870. | 1871. | 1872. | 1873. | 1874. | 1875. | 1876. | 1877. | 1878. | 1879. |
|---|---|---|---|---|---|---|---|---|---|---|
| | £ | £ | £ | £ | £ | £ | £ | £ | £ | £ |
| **Sheep and Cattle Stations—** | | | | | | | | | | |
| Shepherds, married, with double rations.... per annum | 30 | 35 | 37 | 40 | 40 | 40 | 40 | 40 | 40 | 40 |
| " single, and hutkeeper, 1 ration each " | 30 | 35 | 37 | 40 | 40 | 40 | 40 | 40 | 40 | 40 |
| " " keeping own hut, rations. " | 35 | 39 | 40 | 45 | 45 | 50 | 50 | 50 | 50 | 50 |
| Hutkeepers, with rations ............ | 26 | 26 | 26 | 31 | 32 | 32 | 30 | 30 | 36 | 36 |
| Boundary-riders, married, with double rations " | — | — | — | — | — | — | — | 52 | 52 | 52 |
| Lamb-minders, required about 3 months, rations " | 26 | 26 | 31 | 39 | 39 | 39 | 39 | 39 | 39 | 39 |
| Man and wife, with two rations " | 50 | 50 | 52 | 55 | 60 | 65 | 60 | 60 | 60 | 60 |
| Men for general work, rations " | 40 | 40 | 45 | 47 | 50 | 52 | 50 | 50 | 50 | 50 |
| Bush carpenters " | 60 | 60 | 65 | 70 | 78 | 90 | 85 | 90 | 90 | 90 |
| Men cooks " | 45 | 40 | 45 | 52 | 52 | 52 | 52 | 52 | 52 | 52 |
| Teamsters " | 45 | 45 | 45 | 52 | 52 | 52 | 52 | 52 | 52 | 52 |
| Sheepdrovers " | 52 | 52 | 52 | 60 | 60 | 75 | 65 | 65 | 65 | 65 |
| Stockmen " | 55 | 55 | 55 | 60 | 60 | 65 | 60 | 60 | 60 | 60 |
| Coltbreakers " | 55 | 55 | 55 | 60 | 65 | 70 | 70 | 70 | 70 | 70 |
| Water-drawers " | 39 | 39 | 39 | 45 | 45 | 50 | 45 | 45 | 45 | 45 |
| | s. d. | s. d. | s. d. | s. d. | s. d. | s. d. | s. d. | s. d. | s. d. | s. d. |
| Wellsinkers } Average earnings, per week, with rations | 35 0 | 30 0 | 30 0 | 35 0 | 37 0 | 42 0 | 42 0 | 42 0 | 42 6 | 42 6 |
| Hutbuilders } | 30 0 | 30 0 | 30 0 | 35 0 | 39 0 | 40 0 | 40 0 | 40 0 | 40 0 | 40 0 |
| Woolpressers | 35 0 | 30 0 | 30 0 | 30 0 | 30 0 | 30 0 | 35 6 | 35 6 | 35 6 | 35 6 |
| Sheepshearers, average earnings per 100 ........... | 15 0 | 15 0 | 15 0 | 18 0 | 18 0 | 20 0 | 18 6 | 18 6 | 18 6 | 18 6 |
| **Trades, &c.—** | | | | | | | | | | |
| Bakers, with board and lodging ....... per diem | 4 6 | 4 6 | 4 6 | 5 0 | 5 6 | 5 6 | 5 6 | 5 6 | 5 6 | 5 6 |
| Blacksmiths, without board and lodging.... " | 7 6 | 7 6 | 8 0 | 8 6 | 9 0 | 9 0 | 9 0 | 9 0 | 9 0 | 9 0 |
| Bricklayers " " " | 8 0 | 8 0 | 9 0 | 9 0 | 9 0 | 9 0 | 9 0 | 9 0 | 9 0 | 9 0 |
| Brickmakers " per 1,000 | 12 0 | 12 0 | 12 0 | 12 0 | 12 0 | 12 0 | 12 0 | 12 0 | 12 0 | 12 0 |

Bullock-drivers, with rations .......... per annum

| | £40 s. d. | £40 s. d. | £40 s. d. | £52 s. d. | £52 s. d. | £52 s. d. | £52 s. d. | £52 s. d. | £52 s. d. | £52 s. d. |
|---|---|---|---|---|---|---|---|---|---|---|
| Butchers, with board and lodging ...... per diem | 4 6 | 4 6 | 4 6 | 5 0 | 5 0 | 5 0 | 5 0 | 5 0 | 5 0 | 5 0 |
| Cabinetmakers, without board and lodging .. " | 8 0 | 8 0 | 8 0 | 8 0 | 8 0 | 8 0 | 9 0 | 9 0 | 9 0 | 9 6 |
| Carpenters " | 8 0 | 8 0 | 8 0 | 9 0 | 9 0 | 9 0 | 9 0 | 9 0 | 9 0 | 9 0 |
| Carriage-builders " | 9 0 | 9 0 | 9 0 | 9 0 | 9 0 | 9 0 | 8 0 | 8 0 | 8 0 | 8 6 |
| Cigarmakers " | — | — | — | — | — | — | 9 6 | 9 6 | 9 6 | 9 6 |
| Coopers " | 8 0 | 9 0 | 9 0 | 9 0 | 9 0 | 9 0 | 9 6 | 9 6 | 9 6 | 9 6 |
| Collarmakers " | — | — | — | — | — | — | 10 6 | 10 6 | 10 6 | 10 0 |
| Day laborers " | 5 6 | 6 0 | 6 0 | 6 0 | 7 0 | 7 6 | 6 6 | 6 6 | 6 6 | 6 6 |
| French-polishers " | — | — | — | — | 7 6 | — | 7 6 | 7 0 | 7 0 | 7 6 |
| Galvanized iron workers " | — | — | — | — | — | — | 8 0 | 8 0 | 8 0 | 8 0 |
| Harness-makers " | — | — | — | — | — | — | 7 0 | 7 0 | 7 0 | 7 0 |
| Jewellers " | — | — | — | — | — | — | 10 0 | 10 0 | 10 0 | 10 0 |
| Machinists " | 8 0 | 8 6 | 8 6 | 8 6 | 10 0 | 10 0 | 10 0 | 10 0 | 10 0 | 10 0 |
| Masons " | 6 6 | 6 3 | 6 3 | 6 3 | 9 0 | 9 6 | 9 6 | 9 6 | 9 6 | 9 6 |
| Millers " | 6 0 | 9 6 | 9 0 | 9 0 | 9 0 | 9 0 | 9 6 | 9 6 | 9 6 | 9 6 |
| Miners " | 6 0 | 8 6 | 9 6 | 9 6 | 10 0 | 10 6 | 5 0 | 5 0 | 5 0 | 5 0 |
| Painters and glaziers " | 9 0 | 9 6 | 9 6 | 9 6 | 10 0 | 9 6 | 9 0 | 9 0 | 9 0 | 9 0 |
| Plasterers ... per 100 ft. | 6 6 | 6 9 | 6 9 | 6 9 | 10 0 | 10 6 | 10 0 | 10 0 | 10 0 | 10 0 |
| Sawyers ... per diem | 0 9 6 | 0 9 | 6 9 | 6 9 | 7 0 | 7 0 | 7 6 | 7 6 | 7 6 | 7 6 |
| Saddlers " " | 0 8 6 | 0 10 | 0 10 | 0 10 | 0 11 | 0 11 | 1 0 | 1 0 | 1 0 | 1 0 |
| Shoemakers " | — | 8 6 | 8 6 | 8 6 | 8 6 | 8 6 | 8 6 | 8 6 | 8 6 | 7 6 |
| Tailors ... per hour | 8 0 | 8 6 | 8 6 | 8 6 | 7 6 | — | 8 6 | 8 6 | 8 6 | 8 6 |
| Tanners ... per diem | — | — | — | — | — | — | 8 0 | 8 0 | 8 0 | 8 0 |
| Tinsmiths " " | — | — | — | — | — | — | 10 0 | 10 0 | 10 0 | 10 0 |
| Upholsterers " | 8 6 | 9 0 | 9 0 | 9 0 | 9 0 | 9 0 | 9 0 | 9 0 | 9 0 | 9 0 |
| Wheelwrights " | — | — | — | — | — | — | — | — | — | — |

Scale of rations per week—10lbs. flour, 12lbs. meat, 2lbs. sugar, ¼lb tea.
Married farm laborers have cottage provided rent free, and fuel and water gratis.
Servants are conveyed up country at employers' cost.

## Return showing the Wholesale Prices of General Produce in Adelaide in each alternate month of the Year 1879.

| Article | February | | April | | June | |
|---|---|---|---|---|---|---|
| | £ s. d. | £ s. d. | £ s. d. | £ s. d. | £ s. d. | £ s. d. |
| **Flour, Grain, &c.—** | | | | | | |
| Flour ............per ton of 2,000lbs. | 10 10 0 | 10 15 0 | 10 15 0 | 11 0 0 | 11 0 0 | 11 10 0 |
| Wheat ..........per bushel of 60lbs. | 0 4 0 | 0 4 7 | 0 4 9 | 0 4 10 | 0 5 0 | 0 5 1 |
| Bran ............" 20lbs. | 0 0 2 | 0 0 2¼ | 0 1 3 | — | 0 0 3 | 0 1 4 |
| Pollard ........." 20lbs. | 0 1 3 | 0 1 4 | 0 0 4 | — | 0 1 5 | — |
| Oats, N.Z. ......." 40lbs. | 0 4 0 | 0 4 3 | 0 4 0 | — | 0 3 4 | 0 3 6 |
| Barley, Cape ....." 50lbs. | 0 3 6 | 0 3 9 | 0 4 0 | — | 0 4 3 | — |
| " English ......" 50lbs. | *none* | | 0 5 6 | | 0 5 6 | 0 6 6 |
| **Hides, Skins, Bones, &c.—** | | | | | | |
| Hides, Salted ............per lb. | 0 0 2¾ | 0 0 3¼ | 0 0 2¾ | 0 0 3¼ | 0 0 2 | 0 0 2¼ |
| Butchers' Green ..........each | 0 9 0 | 0 10 0 | 0 9 0 | 1 0 0 | 0 10 0 | 0 15 0 |
| Hoofs ..............per ton | 2 0 0 | 2 2 0 | 2 10 0 | 2 10 0 | 0 0 6 | 2 10 0 |
| Green Kangaroo Skins ......per doz. | 0 1 0 | 0 3 0 | 0 1 0 | 0 1 2 | 0 1 6 | 0 0 6 |
| Skins, Calf ............each | 0 0 6 | 0 0 0 | 0 0 6 | 0 2 6 | 0 1 0 | 0 3 0 |
| " Wallaby ............per doz. | 0 10 0 | 1 10 0 | 0 10 0 | 1 0 0 | 0 10 0 | 1 10 0 |
| Shank Bones ............per ton | 5 0 0 | 10 0 0 | 5 0 0 | 10 0 0 | 5 0 0 | 10 0 0 |
| **Bark.—** | | | | | | |
| Wattle, Ground ............per ton | 7 0 0 | 7 10 0 | 7 0 0 | 7 10 0 | 7 10 0 | 7 15 0 |
| " Chopped .............." | 6 0 0 | 6 5 0 | 6 0 0 | 6 5 0 | 6 0 0 | 6 10 0 |
| " Long .............." | 4 10 0 | 5 0 0 | 4 10 0 | 5 0 0 | — | — |

**Tallow, &c.—**
- Fat, Rough ............ per lb.
- " Fine ............ "
- Tallow, Beef, for export ...... per ton
- " Mixed " ...... "
- " Mutton " ...... "

**Wool (South Australian)—**
- Fleece, Scoured, fair ......... per lb.
- Greasy ............ "
- " Inferior and Heavy ....

**Dairy and Farm Produce—**
- Bacon ............ per lb.
- Butter ............ "
- Cheese ............ "
- Eggs ............ per doz.
- Ham ............ per lb.
- Lard ............ "
- Onions ............ per cwt.
- Gum ............ per lb.
- Beeswax ............ "
- Honey ............ "
- Hay ............ per ton
- Maize ............ per bushel
- Prairie Grass ............ "
- Seed, Lucerne ............ per lb.
- Vetches ............ per bushel
- Potatoes ............ per cwt.

F

*Wholesale Prices of General Produce in Adelaide—continued.*

| Article | August | | October | | December | |
|---|---|---|---|---|---|---|
| | £ s. d. | £ s. d. | £ s. d. | £ s. d. | £ s. d. | £ s. d. |
| **Flour, Grain, &c.—** | | | | | | |
| Flour ............ per ton of 2,000lbs. | 12 0 0 | — | 12 0 0 | 12 10 6 | 13 0 0 | 13 5 9 |
| Wheat ........... per bushel of 60lbs. | 0 5 3 | 0 1 2 | 0 5 3 | 0 5 — | 0 5 6 | — |
| Bran ............ " 20lbs. | 0 1 1 | — | 0 1 1 | — | 0 1 2 | — |
| Pollard ......... " 20lbs. | 0 1 4 | 0 0 — | 0 1 4 | 0 0 — | 0 1 4 | — |
| Oats, N.Z. ...... " 40lbs. | 0 3 3 | 0 3 4 | 0 3 3 | 0 3 4 | 0 3 0 | 0 3 3 |
| Barley, Cape .... " 50lbs. | 0 3 6 | 0 3 — | 0 3 6 | 0 3 — | 0 3 4 | 0 3 3 |
| " English .... " 50lbs. | 0 5 6 | 0 6 0 | 0 5 6 | 0 6 0 | 0 5 6 | 0 5 6 |
| **Hides, Skins, Bones, &c.—** | | | | | | |
| Hides, Salted ........... per lb. | 0 0 3 | 0 0 2½ | 0 0 2 | 0 0 2½ | 0 0 2 | 0 0 2½ |
| Butchers' Green ............ each | 0 10 0 | 0 15 0 | 0 10 0 | 0 15 0 | 0 10 0 | 0 15 0 |
| Hoofs ................... per ton | 1 10 0 | 2 10 6 | 1 10 0 | 2 10 6 | 1 10 0 | 2 10 6 |
| Green Kangaroo Skins .... per doz. | 0 0 6 | 0 1 — | 0 0 6 | 0 1 — | 0 0 6 | 0 2 0 |
| Skins, Calf ................ each | 0 1 6 | 0 3 0 | 0 1 6 | 0 3 0 | 0 1 6 | 0 3 0 |
| " Wallaby ......... per doz. | 0 10 0 | 0 10 0 | 0 10 0 | 0 10 0 | 0 10 0 | 0 10 0 |
| Shank Bones ............. per ton | 5 0 0 | 10 0 0 | 5 0 0 | 10 0 0 | 5 0 0 | 10 0 0 |
| **Bark—** | | | | | | |
| Wattle, Ground ......... per ton | 7 10 0 | 7 15 0 | 7 10 0 | 7 15 0 | 7 10 0 | 7 15 0 |
| " Chopped ............ " | 6 0 0 | 6 10 0 | 6 0 0 | 6 10 0 | 6 0 0 | 6 10 0 |
| " Long ............... " | — | — | 4 10 0 | 4 15 0 | 4 10 0 | 4 15 0 |

| | | | | | | | | |
|---|---|---|---|---|---|---|---|---|
| Tallow,— | | | | | | | | |
| Fat, Rough | per lb. | | | | | | | |
| " Fine | | | | | | | | |
| Tallow, Beef, for export | per ton | | | | | | | |
| " Mixed | " | | | | | | | |
| " Mutton | " | | | | | | | |
| Wool (South Australian)— | | | | | | | | |
| Fleece, Scoured, fair | per lb. | | | | | | | |
| Greasy | " | | | | | | | |
| " Inferior and Heavy | " | | | | | | | |
| Dairy and Farm Produce— | | | | | | | | |
| Bacon | per lb. | | | | | | | |
| Butter | " | | | | | | | |
| Cheese | " | | | | | | | |
| Eggs | per doz. | | | | | | | |
| Ham | per lb. | | | | | | | |
| Lard | " | | | | | | | |
| Onions | per cwt. | | | | | | | |
| Gum | " | | | | | | | |
| Beeswax | per lb. | | | | | | | |
| Honey | " | | | | | | | |
| Hay | per ton | | | | | | | |
| Maize | per bushel | | | | | | | |
| Prairie Grass | " | | | | | | | |
| Seed, Lucerne | per lb. | | | | | | | |
| Vetches | per bushel | | | | | | | |
| Potatoes | per cwt. | | | | | | | |

www.ingramcontent.com/pod-product-compliance
Lightning Source LLC
Chambersburg PA
CBHW032237080426
42735CB00008B/897